How the Churches Got to Be the Way they Are

Gavin White

How the Churches
Got to Be
the Way they Are

SCM PRESS
London

TRINITY PRESS INTERNATIONAL
Philadelphia

This edition first published 1990

SCM Press Ltd
26–30 Tottenham Road
London N1 4BZ

Trinity Press International
3725 Chestnut Street
Philadelphia PA 19104

British Library Cataloguing in Publication Data

White, Gavin
How the Churches Got to Be the Way they Are.
1. Christian church. Evangelicanism, history
I. Title
270.8

ISBN 0-334-02487-0

Library of Congress Cataloging-in-Publication Data

White, Gavin.
How the churches got to be the way they are /
Gavin White.
p. cm.
ISBN 0-334-02487-0
1. Church history—18th century. 2. Church history
—19th century. 3. Church history—20th century.
I. Title.
BR475.W45   1991
270.8—dc20   90-41244

Typeset by Gloucester Typesetting Services,
Stonehouse, Glos.
and printed in Great Britain by
Clays Ltd, St Ives Plc, Bungay, Suffolk

Contents

Preface

This book gives a broad view of the movements which have made the modern churches what they are. Only the last two centuries are covered, and this means that most of the movements are part of a single tendency – a tendency to emphasize a happy view of humanity. For that reason the chapters have a certain unity, and something will be lost when single chapters are read on their own. On the other hand, they are intended to be read individually, and certain key facts are introduced into more than one chapter for this reason. I would naturally prefer that everybody should read everything that I have written, but the reader is at liberty to choose.

The text is suitable for students in the last year of their secondary education or their first year at college or university, but it is not really aimed at students as such. Church history is far too interesting to be restricted to those who are preparing for examinations, and a wide variety of readers should gain something from these pages.

Some readers will discover that the facts as they have known them from infancy are treated with scant respect. This is not always my fault, since the story is drawn from a vast number of recent books which the general reader has had no time to read. It has not been possible to mention these books without choking the narrative, but they do exist. On only two subjects, Christmas and Pentecostalism, have I attempted to break new ground, and even there the argument has been hinted at by others.

If some readers find the story as they have known it treated with scant respect, others will find the heroes of the faith, or some of them, treated with equally scant respect. This is perhaps a good thing. Churches do not depend for their life on heroic leaders, though occasionally they have them. Christianity is not just a religion for the heroic few, but a religion for ordinary people with ordinary failings. There are many such in this story. If we are not living in a golden age today, we did not come from one either. Had the churches of the past been better than they were, then their story would not be of use to us.

Lastly, like Christianity and like Christ himself, the story of the churches should be enjoyed and not endured.

The Eighteenth Century

To understand our own century we have to look at the last century, and to understand that we have to look at the century before, which is a never-ending process. But since we are only concerned here with our recent history, we shall only go back to the eighteenth century, which is far enough for most people and too far for some.

It was not all of one lump; no century ever has been. But it had a certain character which will do for our purpose. It was the age of reason. It was very scientific. It believed in natural laws. And while natural laws may sound very right and proper, they can be very painful when used against you. As well as all this, the eighteenth century was the age of Deism, which may have been why it was the age of natural laws. Deism was the belief in a Deity who was not really God in a personal way but was more of a scientific principle.

Relics of that age are still with us. As the pirate is about to be hanged from the yard-arm, he is told, 'Prepare to meet your Maker'. In that century God was considered to be a Maker, and not much more. Creation was his job, and everyone was supposed to be very grateful that he had done his job so well. 'All things bright and beautiful, The Lord God made them all', should have been written in that century, though illogically it was not. 'The spacious firmament on high, With all the blue ethereal sky, And spangled heaven, a shining frame, Their great Original proclaim', did come from that century. You saw God in nature, and very seldom anywhere else. God was the first mover, the Original, the Great Architect, and it is no accident that that was the age of Freemasonry. But the results of that kind of teaching are not all of the best. If God is first and last a Maker, then what happened after? Certainly nothing much which involved God. He might have gone off to a retirement cottage once his contract was completed, and for some Christians he did just that. If God had really made such a wonderful world that it needed no cross and no salvation and no Jesus Christ, except as somebody to point out what a wonderful world God had made, then Jesus Christ was just a moral teacher and no more. In fact he could be less: a teacher of science, if that is less, which it probably is not. Certainly Christ need not be divine and there need be no Holy Spirit except as an impersonal thing like the spirit of progress. So the single person of God was in, and this pushed many towards what we now call Unitarianism. The English Presbyterians in that century virtually all turned Unitarian, and so did most of the Congregationalists in the New England colonies; modern Unitarians are the descendants of one or other of these two groups. This has confused generations of rather dull Anglicans who have assumed that Presbyterianism is only a half-way house on the road to Unitarianism, but we shall see the fruits of this mistake in a later age.

The intellectual climate of the eighteenth century showed itself in science, political economy and religion. In science there was the 'misplaced concreteness' of which the philosopher A. N. Whitehead later complained, and the application of scientific laws which were regarded as unbending until twentieth-century scientists bent them and found that the world still kept turning. In political economy the ideal was to let natural law have free reign without artificial barriers, according to the theories of Adam Smith. Whether there was a sufficiently clear distinction between science and political economy and religion for them to be considered as more than different names for the same thing may be questioned, but if we are to take religion on its own we may find three general approaches. Indeed, we may sometimes find all three approaches in the same person, which is a little confusing.

The first approach was that of the Deists of whom mention has already been made. They are said to have reduced religion to morality and God to a building society, but there was more to their overall view than that. Whether they were reacting against the violence and fanaticism of the wars of religion, or whether they were horrified by the new revelations of seventeenth-century enthusiasm, or whether for more positive reasons, they sought certainty and they sought sobriety. They wanted a God who was impersonal and thus above mere emotion, and they wanted a God whose nature could be proved by observation. Anything else was subjective and emotional and dangerous. It was this basic outlook which caused the French government to impose such severe restrictions on churches as late as the early years of this century, and the Mexican government to do likewise twenty years later, thus leading to civil war.

The second approach was that of the Moderates or Latitudinarians. The latter word is almost enough to damn any movement, but theirs was not only honourable but probably dominant in the churches of the day. They accepted much of the Deist background, but on a key point they differed. They insisted that God was not an impersonal force but a benevolent God, that is, one who was well-wishing towards mankind, and who expected men to love God and love one another in response. To prove their case against the Deists they had to use evidence acceptable to all, which in those days meant evidence drawn from nature, which was then called natural theology. The result was a great deal of scientific writing to prove that every plant and every creature was there to benefit humanity, from which it could be demonstrated that God was really benevolent. On the whole this campaign was successful, but if you steal your enemies' clothes you may end up wearing your enemies' ideas as well, and some of the Moderates came very close to the Deists they were fighting.

The third approach was that of a number of groups who rejected natural religion altogether and relied on revealed religion. Some of these were the sort of people who were later to be known as Evangelicals, though some were not, but none of them made much impact on the bulk of the population. It was very brave of them to reject the prevailing climate of opinion, but it was also quite impractical, for they had no way in which to touch the minds of their fellow-citizens. They were like engineers who have designed a car which will run on a fuel which does not happen to exist, but which may be invented in the future. And yet when the climate of opinion changed, their ideas were available for general use.

Having baldly described the three approaches, I shall now give some examples. The first is the play *Candide* by the French philosopher and writer Voltaire. The play, which is in fact nothing more than an animated tract, is about a young man named Candide whose very name assures the reader that he is a blank page in the book of life, due to be written upon by those around him. Foremost of these is his tutor, a rather preposterous fellow named Pangloss, who keeps insisting that this is the best of all possible worlds. From this it might then be deduced that whoever made it intended it to show his benevolence to all mankind. Unfortunately for Candide, and even for Pangloss, the world is not such a benevolent place, whatever its creator might have had in mind, and Candide undergoes various trials and tribulations as does everyone else in the play. From this we might conclude, and are clearly supposed to conclude, that the creator was not benevolent to mankind, and is impersonal, and should not be worshipped, and so forth.

But if Voltaire produced an argument against the benevolence of whoever or whatever made the world, there were endless attempts to prove the opposite. One came from a clergyman named John Lightfoot, whose sole claim to fame is the authorship of a book published in 1777 and called *Flora Scotica*. This sounds like a novel, but is a textbook of Scottish botany. That he should have written such a work while being a parish clergyman might lead later critics to suppose that he neglected his pastoral work to indulge in secular studies, but in those days no studies could be considered secular, and Lightfoot's intention was religious. His stated aim was to draw readers 'to the rational study of God's works, and the contemplation of his sublime attributes', the most important one being benevolence towards mankind. This is shown by his entry on *cladonia rangiferina*, or reindeer moss, which is only a crude grey blob on a rock, but 'ordained by Providence to be the chief support of the reindeer, and the reindeer of a great part of the inhabitants of the polar regions'. No matter what was studied the result was the same: evidence of God's good will towards mankind.

Of course there were a number of negative reactions against the prevailing climate. David Hume wrote philosophy which was so skeptical that it undermined the faith not only of the orthodox but also of the unorthodox, and in the end it may have left the Deist looking no more reasonable than anyone else. And Methodism, which has always been a bit of a mystery to those who tried to explain its beginnings, may have gained by stressing revealed religion against too much talk of those facts which could be drawn from the study of nature. It is at least tempting to put both Hume and Wesley in the same camp, though admitting that their motives for being there were totally different. But if there were eighteenth-century holders of views which were not typical of that century, there were also holders of eighteenth-century views who did not live in that century. For these views did not disappear entirely in subsequent years. In some people they lived on beneath the surface, a surface given over to nineteenth-century religion, and in other people they were on the surface, like offshore rocks surrounded by a rising tide of what was modern thought. And two such people are worthy of study.

David Livingstone was in many ways an intellectual son of the eighteenth century, which he carried with him to Africa and kept untouched from later thought. He believed in both natural religion, which was known from nature, and in revealed religion, which was not known from nature. And he believed that there was little point in teaching revealed religion until he had laid a solid foundation of natural religion, should this not already exist amongst whatever people he might meet. Thus he was able to write in 1844 about a tribe, 'their depravity being sub-natural, some time elapses ere they are raised to the level of sinners in other countries', meaning that they had no firm grasp on even natural religion. Of another group he said, 'The people have distinctly the idea of a supreme being . . .', and of yet another, 'People assert most positively that of old, before they ever heard of white men, they were in the daily habit of speaking of God and referring certain events to his will.' We may smile at the idea of Livingstone asking Africans if they had any idea of a supreme being, and if they said they had not, then asking them if their ancestors had had any such idea, but he was being reasonable enough within his own limits. And when he found no such idea, Livingstone began to fill the gap. He did this by lecturing 'on the works of God in creation and providence', beginning with 'the goodness of God in giving iron ore', which that people extracted and used.

The second example is that of Ralph Wardlaw, a Scottish Congregationalist who gave Livingstone most of what theological teaching he was to receive. In 1812 Wardlaw's brother was killed at the battle of Salamance, and he marked the occasion with a sermon called *The Doctrine of a Particular Providence*. He argued that anyone who believed in God must accept 'a superintending providence', but, and this was the controversial point, providence was 'not general only but particular'. This took the theology of the benevolent God a stage farther: God was benevolent not only in setting up the world but in intervening for particular purposes, and it was this as much as anything which distinguished the coming Evangelical from his forebears. Some have thought, continued Wardlaw, 'that the necessity of a particular providence may be superseded, by supposing a perfect original arrangement of the universal system', and Wardlaw was enough of an eighteenth-century thinker to accept this for 'the material universe'. But it would not do for people, since it was 'quite too mechanical'. For them God had other and more surprising ways of acting, and though events such as the death of his brother might suggest a less than benevolent deity, 'there exists in the mind of God a reason for every part of his conduct'.

The eighteenth century left a mixed legacy to the nineteenth. There was the quite extraordinary emphasis on the creation. There was a vacuum which was to be filled by the renewed interest in the salvation of mankind by Christ. There was a heady optimism which assumed that with a bit of organization and the right sort of rules anything wrong in the world could be put right. And if relics of the prevailing thought of the eighteenth century lasted in the backs of people's minds in later days, there were also pockets of society and pockets of geography in which eighteenth-century ideas remained at the forefront. It has even been suggested that working-class popular religion in Victorian England was the moral religion of the well-meaning God of the eighteenth century, without sin or salvation, transmitted under the noses of the clergy by working-class teachers in Sunday schools. But perhaps it is fairer to say that the religious outlook of the eighteenth century is an aspect of religion in any age, though only in the eighteenth century was it dominant.

Evangelicals

There have probably been Evangelicals in every age of history and Evangelicals of some sort in every world religion. It is as much a way of thought and a way of living as anything else. But what makes the Evangelical what he is? There is no simple answer which will satisfy everyone, but if we look at those Evangelicals who lived at the end of the eighteenth century we find a word which they use. That word is 'surprise'. They believed in surprises. Everyone else believed in a set pattern of causes and effects, which were all worked out by processes coming from the first force long ago, and which were interlocked by something called economy, which was not what we would call economy. But Evangelicals believed that this process was interrupted by surprises. God intervened, suddenly, unexpectedly. The ordinary process of cause and effect was, in Wardlaw's words, 'quite too mechanical'. So a short definition of an Evangelical is someone who does not believe in cause and effect, it being understood that nowadays almost nobody believes in cause and effect as they used to do.

Evangelical magazines of the day show this clearly. They are an interesting mix of poetry, exhortation, book notes and death-bed scenes. They are generally intelligent and reasonable, but they suddenly go berserk when they want to show that God intervenes. A ship is bearing down on the rocks, the look-out is asleep, all reasonable probability is that there will be an almighty smash. But effect does not follow cause, for someone is distracted by some apparently accidental happening and wanders along the deck, looks casually over the bow, calls out in alarm, and just in time the ship is brought on to the other tack and avoids the danger. A proliferation of dignitaries descends upon Cambridge to elect a head of college, and it is clear that one man, and none other, will be elected. But one of the electors travels by a coach which loses a wheel, and he has to wait at the roadside while the election swings to an un-expected conclusion. A dissolute waster lies dying, after a life of selfish-ness and worse. At the last moment he calls his friends together to perform an act of generosity. In those days death-bed scenes were popular outside Evangelical circles, since death was much in the public mind when so many children failed to outlive their childhood, and adults might fail at any time. Children were asked to prepare for death, which seems grotesque to us, but many of those who were asked to prepare for death actually died in childhood. So Evangelicals stressed the surprising aspects of death-beds, even while they tried to encourage appropriate death-bed scenes as examples to others, and editors asked for authentic stories. If the stories of sudden intervention in Evangelical literature tell us anything, it is that God intervenes in Christ to save mankind. The slow ticking of the great clock which is the world is interrupted and something happens. There is a story of an Evangelical vicar parachuted into a Church of England parish by its patron, and at first preaching on the benevolence of God until he was accepted by his flock and could then preach about the cross. Which no doubt he did. Often. And at length.

There is a tendency to portray the Evangelicals as standing four-square against all the heresies of the Enlightenment, by which title all the different ideas of the eighteenth century are conveniently lumped into one enemy. A more convincing view is that of D. W. Bebbington who argues that 'Evangelicalism was allied to the Enlightenment', and shows that there was a parallel between Evangelical thinkers and Locke who taught the appeal to experience. If this is true it makes more sense of the whole movement, and shows it providing a way in which Christ-ians could live their faith in an age dominated by Enlightenment ideas. In Bebbington's words, 'The Evangelical version of Protestantism was created by the Enlightenment'.

From 1790 until about 1820 Evangelicals were a very mixed bunch. Most of them had grown up on creation and benevolence religion, and they would revert to this from time to time. But there were also a lot of new ideas floating around, and Evangelicals could be pietistic, moralis-tic, apocalyptic, or sacramentalist. In fact a great many were sacra-mentalist, and their death-bed scenes brought this out in surprising ways. Few were puritanical in life-style. There is a story of a noted Evangelical family in which novels were not permitted, though there was one, by Sir Walter Scott, in the house; it had come from the original Evangelical of the dynasty who read all Scott's novels as they appeared. The gloomy picture of Evangelical life which has come to us from later novels does not fit the early pioneers, who were full of bounce and cheerfulness, and it was probably exaggerated even with regard to the later Evangelicals when a certain fortress mentality had set in.

Evangelicalism was a lay movement, unlike Methodism, and in some ways it was a commercial movement. This does not mean that it was a cloak for money-making; it means that it had a lot of merchants in it, and they could exercise little influence in the church as they were neither patrons nor parsons. Instead, they used the structures they knew best, and these were companies. Early Evangelical societies had the same organization, and to some extent still do, as companies to sell fish or weave cloth. There were literally hundreds of such companies; William Wilberforce was on the board of about forty of them. There were societies to reform cab-drivers, to reclaim coster-mongers, to distribute tracts to crossing-sweepers, to provide medical care for the poor, and to bury the dead. It has been suggested that the works of mercy were only meant to bring the lost to a place where they could be converted, but the evidence is that the Evangelical social conscience was active in its own right. And Evangelicals worked with infidels as well as the faithful, where the aims were solely of this world.

They were not revolutionaries. They believed in working in society from the top down. To this day an older Evangelical society will have on its board one minor member of the aristocracy, one retired major-general, and one All-England cricketer. The connection with sport is perhaps accidental and dates from a later period, and the connection with taking of the waters at Bath, Cheltenham, Harrogate, Crieff, or wherever mineral waters could be found, was probably no more signi-ficant than the fact that this type of religion and that type of therapy both arose at the same time. Yet if the Evangelicals had little sense of social reform, it must be noticed that neither had anyone else in their day. They picked up some of the cast-offs of a diabolical society without thinking that they could change that society; most people did not even do that.

They were All-British. In 1795 the union of certain English and Scottish Evangelicals led some zealot to proclaim that the political union of 1707 had now been extended to matters religious, and that differences between the Church of England and the Church of Scotland would soon disappear. In fact there were enthusiasts who hoped to replace both establishments with a radical Congregationalism, and this led the General Assembly in Scotland to produce a 'Pastoral Admonition' against such travelling preachers in 1799. The great bulk of Scottish Evangelicals supported this Pastoral Admonition, and churchly Evangelicalism became the norm in Scotland. Something less marked happened in England in 1799, but if Scottish Evangelicals argued in later days for the church against the state, and against lay patrons, in England the Evangelicals often were the lay patrons and were resisting High Churchmen and relying on a lay parliament to keep the clergy in check. They developed a mystique of Crown and Nobility and Parliament, all guaranteeing the Reformation Settlement and the 1662 Prayer Book, selectively interpreted, against any assumed novelty. Only since the 1960s has English Evangelicalism abaondoned this defensive reliance on the past, which it no longer needs.

William Wilberforce is usually described as the main figure in early British Evangelicalism and his approach is summed up in the title of his book, published in 1797, *A Practical View of the Prevailing Religious System of Professed Christians in the Higher and Middle Classes in this Country contrasted with Real Christianity*. It was practical always, concerned with the upper ranks of society (the lower classes would be dealt with by legislation rather than persuasion), and distinguishing between what passed for Christianity and what really was. It is well known that Wilberforce and his colleagues struggled against slavery, and it is also well known that this was not the only evil in their day. But it was an evil that merchants knew, and it was one that John Newton knew, he having been in the slave-trade before his conversion, though his constant harping on his earlier sins was somewhat exaggerated. Perhaps he was obliged to remind himself of his earlier weaknesses lest he became complacent. Hannah More is a third figure of note, exceptional in being of humble origin, a great founder of Sunday schools, and a writer of tracts. These had an enormous influence even if they could not always convince the critical reader. Her story of the poor shepherd, for instance, might have been more striking had not the shepherd's constant assertions of his contentment at living in poverty led to his being taken out of that beloved poverty. But what is most amazing is that two million copies of this tract were distributed in a single year, when England had but nine million people. This was only to be surpassed by the massive printings of Sunday school tracts and texts in the nineteenth century, when the vast bulk of printed matter must have been religious.

It is sometimes asserted that the Evangelicals brought Britain back from vice and frivolity into an age of seriousness. There was such an age, and we may see the change in the novels of Georgette Heyer and those of Anthony Trollope. In the latter, Archdeacon Grantly in the bishop's palace says he remembers whist being played in a room, whereupon the bishop's wife says she hopes it will never be played there again. The Archdeacon's wife later scolds her husband, 'You know very well,' she says, 'that the times are changed, and if you were Bishop of Barchester you would not have played whist in the palace.' Was this because of Evangelicalism? Probably not; the Archdeacon was no Evangelical. And everyone became serious, whether they were Evangelical, High Church, Latitudinarian, Dissenter, Roman Catholic, or atheist. And if we still meet the argument that Evangelicals made everyone else serious without usually making them Evangelical, this does not explain how Evangelicals who were devout but not serious in the late eighteenth century became serious to the point of stodginess as the nineteenth century got into its stride. Probably Evangelicalism and seriousness were quite different things, but whether seriousness was a good thing or a bad thing is another question. On the whole, it must have been a welcome development, but it could be taken to extremes and sometimes was.

America looms large in the history of Evangelicalism. Jonathan Edwards, America's sole theologian, may not have had the same influence at home which he acquired abroad, and his Calvinist stress on God's action never stopped Americans acting themselves, for Edwards did put morality firmly in the centre. In due course the Calvinism faded. As in Britain, this was most notably in the 1830s, when Charles Finnie flourished as an evangelist of God's grace to all, and then in the 1870s, when Dwight L. Moody had a similar message and, in the prevailing climate of thought, was widely successful. And in Moody's teaching the emphasis on making a decision for Christ would have been quite impossible had there still been a Calvinist culture. But the morality remained, and this may be why American Evangelicalism is even more related to slavery than is British Evangelicalism. The impression was given that Christian religion in America revolved around the issue of slavery, and that in later days it was a reaction to the aftermath of slavery. Revivalists revived against slavery. Denominations split over slavery. If you were right on slavery you were right on religion, and if you were wrong on slavery you were wrong on everything else. If the country finally divided on slavery, the churches divided first, and the Evangelicals led the way.

But there were two distinct 'awakenings' in American Evangelicalism. The First Awakening came in the eighteenth century, and the Second in the nineteenth. Some would date this Second Awakening from as early as 1811 and events at Yale University, while others would date it from

1859, when there was a stock-market crash in New York and stock-brokers wandered dazedly about in the streets until a helpful janitor opened the doors of a church and they flocked in to pray. This Second Awakening was not led by ministers as much as by businessmen and claimed to be practical in its impatience with theology. When Moody visited Britain in 1873 he did so as a businessman in a business suit, and asked his hearers to decide for Christ. It was assumed that people could make such a choice, and that there was nothing to stop them. Of course this offended old-fashioned Evangelicals with their Calvinist views of sin, who were doubtful about souls being turned around in a moment. Moody referred to Highland Scots who claimed that it took six months for salvation to be effective, and said that a man could be dead and damned before that time had elapsed. When a Highlander tried to argue with him, Moody promised to pray for him, which annoyed the Highlander, who said that with his theology Moody should have the Highlander praying for him and not the other way round. But gradually the Second Awakening, in Britain as in America, overcame the teachings of the First Awakening. And one of the less happy results was a cheerful expectation that if there was enough faith and enough prayer and enough work, then conversion must result. Nobody could resist, for human nature was not capable of holding out against evangelism, and if it did hold out, then there must be some fault in the evangelism. Which, of course, may have been the effect of a Calvinist view of human nature and powerlessness operating beneath the surface of a non-Calvinist Evangelicalism.

Yet nothing is static, not even this. In the 1950s British and American and other Evangelicals underwent a renewal with a loosening of old restraints. There came to be a variety of new forms of Evangelicalism, some of which would not have been recognized by an older generation, and some of which were not recognized by each other. These new ventures have led to the claim that Evangelicalism has come back from the dead and is gradually replacing every other form of Christianity or so-called form of Christianity. Evangelicalism may well have walked out of the geriatric hospital, but it is only remarkable in comparison with what it was. In the world spectrum of Christianity it waxes and wanes like everything else.

- 3 -

Gothic Revival

In the middle of the last century there was a radical change in Western thought; this probably reached its peak in the spring of 1843. It was a shift from the direct to the indirect, from knowing something to knowing something which might tell you about something else. It came to be assumed that direct knowledge was impossible, and truths could only be grasped by their effects as seen in nature, in culture, and in words. In art there was an outburst of romanticism and much painting of ruined castles and waterfalls and stags on mountain tops, all of which meant something very deep. In music there was a decline of straightforward melodies in favour of complicated works which zoomed all over. In literature Sir Walter Scott had already led the way, but poetry was suddenly popular as metre and rhyme hid the truth from all but the most determined of readers. In household furnishings all sorts of useless articles obscured the plain lines of furniture and it was this, rather than mere prudery, which caused trousers to be stitched on to table legs. But it was in architecture that the Gothic Revival was most obvious.

Gothic Revival architecture was not just Gothic. The instinct to break up the lines of buildings caused simple box-like dwellings in the American South to have verandahs wrapped around them like crinoline dresses. But for what was truly Gothic, the high priest was A. W. Pugin, who claimed that you could not convert England to Christianity with pagan, by which he meant Greek or Roman classical, architecture. He even had doubts about the religious views of a friend who had incorrect Gothic shapes to his windows; incorrect Gothic led to incorrect thinking. For the Houses of Parliament in London he designed Gothic inkwells, thus encouraging parliamentarians to write their letters in a Christian frame of mind, or at least a Christian frame of ink. Sir Gilbert Scott presented a Gothic design for a new Foreign Office, which might have led to a Christian foreign policy, though in fact they accepted a Byzantine design. Whether that led to a Byzantine foreign policy must be left to the historians.

There were Gothic railway stations, Gothic prisons, Gothic bakeries and Gothic horse troughs, though no Gothic horses. In New York there were plans for a Gothic elevated railway, though happily they came to nothing. And there was Gothic writing, which still identifies church signboards in many countries. But Gothic buildings were favoured not just because they came from a Christian era of history, but because they produced a dim religious light. The altar of a church was seen through a screen, and down a long tunnel. It was shrouded like a nuclear reactor. The unworthy never came near enough to the holy to desecrate it, and it never came near enough to do them an injury. There was an uproar when Londoners learned that a railway bridge was to be built over the street leading to St Paul's Cathedral, but in fact they learned to appreciate the view of the Cathedral seen through a screen of railway signals. And in the same period it was thought that art should imitate nature. Nature was both a screen between us and God, and a means of showing what God was like, so Gothic imitated the lines of trees in a forest, rather than the mere mathematics of squares and circles in Greek and Roman buildings.

In religion this was called 'reserve'. The faith should not be directly displayed to the unfaithful, but taught through symbols. Direct preaching was useless since people did not learn directly. Christianity could only be known through a Christian culture, and through a Christian church. John Keble expressed this in a hymn, 'The moon above, the Church below, A wondrous race they run; But all their radiance, All their glow, Each borrows of its Sun.' God would be, in the words of another hymn, 'remote, inaccessible, hid from our eyes', only to be revealed, like the black holes of astronomy, by effects on neighbouring objects,

But for all its distancing of God, the movement believed in a God who was actively at work. The eighteenth century believed in a God who did everything at the creation, the Evangelicals in a God who did everything on the cross, the churchmen of the 1840s in a God working through the church. This meant that the church was immensely important, and must be free from state control, which led to a century of conflict with theories of the state. Again, if God worked through the church, so also through sacraments, which not only expressed God but expressed him in cultural forms. And God worked through the clergy, who became increasingly separate from the laity as their status and their function changed.

That this was a world-wide shift in emphasis has not always been recognized. There are still some who believe that it all began at Oxford, and spread outwards, but these are usually people who believe that everything begins at Oxford. Had they not been riding on the crest of a wave, the Oxford leaders would now be remembered as just a few more of the eccentrics so common in that place. For in the same years we are told that in County Beauce, in the backwoods of Quebec, 'le bon Dieu', the old God of benevolence, was replaced by a more demanding God. In Montreal the bishop went to great lengths to change the headgear of his clergy. In New York the bishop struggled to end lay control of church buildings. In Mexico a new wave of Catholicism evangelised the western areas, and it was a new form of Catholicism too. And none of these people knew or cared of Oxford.

It is sometimes suggested that Roman Catholics in Ireland had to conform to English Catholic customs in those years. But it is also said that Roman Catholics in England had to conform to Italian Catholic ways, though nobody has said to what ways Italian Catholics had to conform. There is a famous story of an English visitor to Rome just before the shift in emphasis who asked who might be in a rather splendid carriage driving by. He was shocked to learn that this was the Pope, as nobody paid much attention. But the Pope was soon to become a rather distant figure on a balcony, guarded from too close a view. Everywhere Roman Catholics changed, and if opponents charged that this was a plot to give more power to the clergy, the truth is that the laity wanted these changes and sometimes the clergy were slow to accept them.

In any event, it was not confined to Roman Catholics and Anglicans. It swept through the Lutheran world as well, with the Missouri Synod being the most notable example derived from a theocratic community of Saxon migrants which emerged in precisely the critical years. In English Congregationalism Thomas Binney led a high-church movement at King's Weigh House, while in Methodism the churchly innovations of Jabez Bunting were part of the wider tendency. In Scotland the Disruption of 1843 resulted from the demand for spiritual independence from the state. The Catholic Apostolic Church was formed on the basis of an immense number of orders of the ministry, a splendid sacramental order, speaking in tongues, and the immediate expectation of the Second Coming. Finally, there was the emergence of the Brethren (or Plymouth Brethren), who were opposed to state interference, had an active sacramental life, and produced a dispensational wing. Dispensationalists saw progress in stages comparable to those of the Adventists, another 1840s movement, and to Marxism, which might most usefully be studied in conjunction with its more religious birthmates. The new wave could not be ignored, and those who tried to do so found themselves out of touch with their age and condemned to dwindle away.

The story of the Church of England is best known, though the change which began with the Oxford Movement has perhaps been exaggerated. There were high churchmen before those of Oxford, though it suited the younger zealots to paint their forefathers in the darkest of hues. Nonetheless, the change was most evident in the Church of England, though why this should have been so is still something of a mystery. It is said that Platonic philosophy with its view of ideas concealed behind a veil was a factor in England. This might have been so had the vast bulk of the English people had a chance to learn Platonic philosophy or anything else. It is said that in the preceding century the state had crippled the legislative machinery of the Church of England and so left it unable to resist change, but government might have prevented that change had it had popular support in so doing. It is said that after the political reforms of 1832 the bishops votes' in the House of Lords were no longer important to the state, so they became a focal point for church reform, but in fact the bishops were decidedly unwilling to be a focal point for anything and leadership was thrust upon them. The question remains but the answers do not.

What is clear is that things came to a head through political pressure to reform the Church of England and sweep away all that was not useful, which meant most of it. Cathedrals were a particular target for reformers, which led Churchmen into the most tortuous arguments to show their utility. The one convincing argument, that they attracted tourists, still lay in the future. But even while politicians, full of new theories of state sovereignty over everything there was, prepared to take on the church, a Tory government set up an Ecclesiastical Commission which from 1836 onwards applied most of the revenues of the Church of England according to need. As one example, the dean and canons of Durham, who enjoyed vast incomes, were required to devote their wealth to the founding of a new university which still sports their portraits as a tribute to their generosity. In such ways the threat of more state interference was blunted, but strict churchmen resented even that much state activity, and in 1833 Parliament had already taken one step which offended.

They had suppressed ten bishoprics of the Church of Ireland, then linked to the Church of England. Ireland had a large number of bishoprics, deaneries, and canonries, largely used for government patronage and financed by tithes raised from a predominantly Roman Catholic population. Nobody could deny that they needed to be suppressed, and only Parliament could have done it, but it was a precedent for Parliament suppressing whole churches. So in that year John Keble preached in a service for judges at Oxford, astonishing any of those gentry who were listening by condemning the nation for its apostasy. Keble was then a tutor at Oriel College, and later a country vicar, a rather saintly figure though perhaps not quite of this world. He is best remembered for his poetry, in which he conveyed religious truths somewhat in the spirit of the organizer of a children's party who hides prizes in the flower beds.

In the same year a Cambridge don named Hugh James Rose gathered some friends at his Suffolk rectory to form an 'Apostolical' party of churchmen who would lean more on the apostles than on Parliament. Rose was the sort of person who had learned Greek by the age of five, and he was one of the two Church of England men who knew German biblical scholarship, though he did nothing with it. He died young of tuberculosis; it was this disease which took him to Rome for a winter, where he may have been influenced by John Henry Hobart, Episcopal Bishop of New York, also there for his health (nervous stomach), and a living example of a bishop unconnected with any state. Rose later drifted apart from the Oxford men, as did W. H. Hook, who was later famous for putting Oxford Movement ideas into practice at Leeds Parish Church. As a curate in the Isle of Wight, Hook had travelled half across England to meet Hobart, who was making an early visit to England. He was duly astonished at the shape of his hat.

But the most notable of the Oxford men was John Henry Newman, a delicate soul, a man of remarkable intellect, and yet all too like the girl in the song who went into the garden to eat worms. Of extreme evangelical background, he had little sense of the Church of England, and when he turned from that body he might equally well have become Roman Catholic, as he did, or Plymouth Brethren, as his brother did. As a fellow of Oriel he was much influenced by Hurrell Froude, who threw out all sorts of ideas which were taken up by both Newman and Keble before Froude's early death through the usual tuberculosis. Newman was a thinker with excellent antennae; he picked up topical themes and expressed them in his theology. His first major work on the development of Christian doctrine, to justify Catholic teachings, applied the 1840s ideas of change and development to doctrine as Darwin applied them to species. On the other hand, his idea of Protestantism was a mere caricature and as he lacked any idea of corruption to place beside that of development, he had to argue that Protestantism was scarcely Christian at all and developed from something else. In so far as he used the early heresy of Arianism (denying the divinity of Christ) to typify Protestantism or Presbyterianism, and Semi-Arianism to typify Anglicanism halfway down the slippery slope, he may well have been misled by a belief that Presbyterians really were Arians. In later years he referred to Presbyterians as if he meant Unitarians, and this was an old English confusion caused by English Presbyterians having largely become Unitarian in the eighteenth century. In his other great work, on the *Grammar of Assent*, Newman caught up and expressed the idea of choice which was dominant in the 1870s. But throughout this man's story there are recurrent fits of gloom, depression and uncertainty.

Newman was the principle writer of the Tracts from which the Tractarians got their name, though Isaac Williams and Robert Wilberforce actually produced the most thoughtful ones. Between them they set out the whole doctrine of a church essentially independent of the state and grounded on apostolic authority exercised by bishops. In fact few English bishops saw themselves in such terms, and when the Bishop of Oxford spoke mildly against the new ways Newman was taken aback and withdrew from active work. So began the long succession of steps which by 1845 led him into the Roman Catholic Church. One historian quotes his last sermon in the Church of England which, he complained, 'biddest them (her sons) stand all the day idle . . . or thou biddest them be gone . . . or thou sellest them for naught to the stranger that passes by'. And that historian adds, 'Two years later the stranger bought him, and eyed his bargain with suspicion.' Yet tales of Roman Catholic insensitivity to Newman tell only half of the story.

Leadership in Oxford fell to E. B. Pusey, who was the other man in the Church of England who had tasted German theology and, unlike Rose, had first thought well of it. If Pusey's toughness and his conservativism were too much for his opponents, it was partly because he hated to change anything, because he believed so strongly that whatever is seen is only a veil for whatever there is, and any change might have unforeseen consequences. You never could know what unseen truth might lie behind it, and be for ever swept away. It was this outlook which made adherents of all the movements of the 1840s so conservative about the Bible; their devotion to the exact text made them appear similar to the Fundamentalists of a later era, but in fact it arose from diametrically opposite beliefs. The Fundamentalists were to believe that the text of the Bible was the Bible, while those of the 1840s believed that it was a key which might unlock the mysteries of the Bible.

By by the 1850s the Oxford Movement was at work in parish churches as well as in Oxford: first in a church where the vicar shocked people by wearing his white surplice for the sermon instead of changing to a black gown; then in a church where they marked Christmas by decorating with green boughs; then in a church where the vicar had his wife sew together two Oxford academic hoods to make a passable priestly garment for the Eucharist; and step by step, changes in worship reflected the new emphasis in teaching. Those who were ahead of the herd in moving to a more sacramental life were called 'high', and those who were behind were called 'low', which did not necessarily mean Evangelical. Virtually no parish remained unaffected.

The diary of Francis Kilvert, a country curate on the borders of Wales, is full of such things. He was no radical, and was shocked at the goings-on of an 'advanced' church in Oxford, but in the early 1870s he recorded various signs of progress in his own area. He visited the ruins of St David's Cathedral, which were being restored; without the Gothic Revival no one would have thought of doing such a thing. His own church was decorated with green boughs for the first time. The squire consented to having all the Holy Communion service taken at the altar, instead of the first part being taken from the reading desk down in the chancel. An old woman received the sacrament for the first time at the age of ninety; a previous generation would have let her go on as she was. And an old man marvelled, 'I do often ponder when I lie in bed, and last night I was thanking God that the Blessed Sacrament has come through all the broils for eighteen hundred years.' In earlier days he might have spoken of things religious, but probably not of the sacrament, and not of it coming through the broils from apostolic times. In that period it was suddenly common to see things religious in terms of sacraments, and even to see sacraments in terms of broils, the unknown by the known.

4

The Second Spring

The 'Second Spring' was a term used by Newman to describe the revival of English Roman Catholicism after the long winter which set in
at the Reformation. But it was probably a misleading term, since there
was no return to the Middle Ages. Instead, there was an adjustment to
the new climate of ideas known as the Gothic Revival, which tended to
favour Roman Catholicism. And there are three reasons for this having
happened.

The first is that Roman Catholics were already more sacramental than
others, and this is partly true. But in adjusting to the previous climate,
that of the eighteenth century, they had minimized the sacramental.
They had become urbane and unromantic. They had introduced into
the framework of the mass prayers like those of the Non-conformists,
and their preaching was as concerned with the Deist threat as that of
everyone else. In the 'Cisalpine Club', which offset Roman claims with
concerns from beneath the Alps, or on this side of the Alps, there was a
half-formed tendency to place Roman Catholicism alongside the Church
of England, with its own Book of Common Prayer. There was practical
recognition of the oversight of the Catholic gentry, and sometimes of
the local Protestant gentry, while church buildings were frequently held
by lay trustees. Nobody thought of the conversion of England to
Catholicism. And yet the mass was there, and so was the papacy, ready
to be given primacy in the later nineteenth century.

The second reason is that, in an era when church and state were to be
quite separate, Roman Catholicism was quite separate. This separation
had previously been unwelcome; English Roman Catholics always
wanted some form of state recognition, and Rome assumed that the
answer to the English problem was a Catholic king. But after the 1840s
Roman Catholics in England had an enormous advantage over English

Anglicans and Scottish Presbyterians who were struggling to escape the embrace of the state, and also over continental Catholics whose bishops were habitually state nominees, and where establishment was as much a fact of history as in Great Britain. Yet it must be admitted that state oversight was everywhere more of a theological burden than a practical one. The English Jesuit who claimed that the Church of England was a department of state 'like the Post Office' was out of touch with reality, though in an age of romanticism it was sometimes an advantage to be out of touch with reality.

The third reason is Irish immigration into England. There is now a lively debate as to whether Ireland provided England with devout Catholics, or with a godless rabble who had to be re-converted by English Roman Catholics. In fact it was probably neither. Ireland provided England with potential Roman Catholics, who were Catholic by identity and tradition but Catholic in an archaic sense. They had to be given a more modern form of Catholicism before they could become active, but most did not need to be re-converted. Of course many were never given this modern form of Catholicism, and many fell away altogether, but the figures give the overall story. There were 54,000 English Roman Catholics in 1780, which was a decline from the previous generation, a decline due to indifference and not to persecution, which had virtually faded away. But by 1840 there were 450,000, which was 2.8 per cent of the population; and by that date there were 420,000 Irish-born in England, of whom the vast majority were Catholic. By the 1851 census there were 700,000 Roman Catholics in England, although only 252,000 showed up at mass, but they were enough to launch Roman Catholicism on the national scene, and the Irish were assimilated relatively painlessly. One writer has noted that in areas such as East Anglia where the Irish never settled, '. . . Catholicism is still almost extinct to-day'.

Like the Church of England, English Catholicism changed its worship. The Mass became a corporate act, and not just the backdrop to personal devotions. It has been noted that the traditional English Catholic devotional book, Challoner's *Garden of the Soul*, was intended for private meditation, but in this period was re-written as 'a liturgical guide to attendance at Mass'. Missionaries from Italy were introduced, and shocked older Catholics by blessing medals, while Gothic vestments were described by one bishop as 'most frightful'. A seminary president wrote of a retreat, a spiritual exercise, as 'solitary confinement for ten days in darkened rooms, I do not think I can go through with it'. But if conservative Catholics were shocked, the new devotions met the needs of the new age, and there was no turning back, at least until the 1960s, when the clock had to be wound up again.

Yet the most astonishing thing about English Roman Catholics in this period was their obsession with the Church of England. If Rome was obsessed with England, and saw England as the land which would not only save the Papal States from Italian nationalists but would also be a vehicle for spreading the Catholic faith throughout the world, Rome shared with English Catholics the idea that the key to the conversion of England was the Church of England. There were a very few who thought of corporate reunion, but the vast majority sought individual conversions which would leave the Church of England as an empty shell. Year after year they predicted the great crisis which would send all the Catholic-minded Anglicans scurrying to Rome, and year after year the crisis failed to occur. It was calculated that around 1850, when conversions were at their height, there were only about 1,400 or 1,500 a year, which meant eighty-three persons each year for every million non-Catholics in the country. Of course it could be argued that converts were mainly from the upper classes, and would thus lead to many more converts from the general population, but this never happened. Instead Roman Catholics spent much time taking the pulse of the Church of England to see when they might inherit its estate, without realizing that what ailed the Church of England was an external factor which was later to afflict the bedside observer as well as the patient. But that external factor, if it was secularism, only came much later; what troubled the Church of England in the middle of the nineteenth century was its state connection.

In fact Roman Catholics were ill-served by enthusiastic converts who reported that the heart of the Church of England *was* its state connection, Newman being a leading promoter of this fancy. And converts were far too ready to predict the imminent conversion of all really serious Anglicans, by whom they meant their own best friends. Yet there was also a belief that Anglicanism had in it some undefined principle which was hostile to Catholicism and was ultimately stronger than Catholicism, so that rigid separation was essential. As if such ideas were not enough, or more than enough, there was yet another fantasy at work. Roman Catholic arguments against the validity of Anglican ordinations were partly due to an unwillingness to leave Anglicans where they were, but there was also a fear of blasphemy. If Anglican priests really were priests, then the sacramental elements of bread and wine were in danger of irreverent treatment, and improbable tales circulated in Roman Catholic circles about what was done to the remaining elements once the service was over.

Finally, there was a tendency amongst certain intellectual Roman Catholics to associate Protestantism with Capitalism. Of course this was not limited to them, nor is it today, but it enabled them to blame all the ills of industrial society on Luther and Calvin. This meant that if England ever did become Catholic, then the slums and the horrors of the factories would be replaced by a more humane and brotherly social system, such as was believed to have existed in the Middle Ages. And if Roman Catholics had little effect on social thought in England and contributed little to political life, it may well have been because so many of them thought that all social problems could be solved by converting more Anglicans.

The main figure of the 'Second Spring' was Nicholas Wiseman, who had been born in Spain of an Irish family, was long in Rome, and who arrived in England in 1835 saying, 'I intend to quarter myself on such of the nobility or gentry of these realms as can sufficiently appreciate such an honour ...'. He became Vicar Apostolic, a bishop without formal status, first for the Midlands and then for London; Pugin designed St Chad's Cathedral in Birmingham largely for his sermons. When a regular hierarchy of bishops was established by Rome in 1850, Wiseman was made the first Archbishop of Westminster and Cardinal, and issued a flamboyant pastoral letter saying, amongst other indiscretions, 'we govern and shall continue to govern the counties of Middlesex, Hereford, and Essex ...'. Although any sensible reader would understand that these words only referred to spiritual oversight of Roman Catholics in those counties, they were taken to be a challenge to the state. The uproar was extraordinary, and Lord John Russell, the Prime Minister, wrote foolishly against Roman Catholics and 'papal aggression'. Parliament weakly passed an Ecclesiastical Titles Act refusing to allow the use of territorial titles by bishops, though Rome had carefully avoided using titles already used by Anglicans and thus had acted within the law. The only long-term result was to antagonize the Irish Catholic supporters of Russell's government, and to bring that government down, while losing one of the few opportunities to provide justice and peace in Ireland.

Anti-Popery agitation in Britain has always been something of a mystery. It is common enough to say that this harks back to deep-seated memories of persecution by Queen Mary Tudor and 'the fires of Smithfield', but this does not take into account those periods in English history when there has been little or no anti-Popery. More particularly, if there was a folk-memory of the sixteenth century behind nineteenth-century episodes of anti-Catholicism, then this does not explain good relations during the eighteenth century. In fact the whole 'fires of Smithfield' approach assumes a collective unconscious and a good deal of Jungian psychology, and without this the whole theory falls to the ground. In any event, the origins of anti-Popery may have been varied. On the one hand there was mere anti-clericalism, mixed with a modernist suspicion of religion of any sort as unprogressive. On the other hand, anti-Popery may have been linked to nationalism and the belief that by claiming independence for their church the Roman Catholics, and indeed Catholic-minded Anglicans, were being disloyal to the Queen and to their fellow-citizens. Certainly British anti-Catholicism flourished in the same periods as continental anti-Catholicism, and it seems that the key decades of this agitation, the 1850s, the 1890s and the 1920s, were those in which racial or national identity were up for re-examination. Finally, there is a possible relationship between anti-Catholicism and anti-Semitism, in so far as both groups were seen to be outside the national community, but popular prejudice opposed Catholics as they were thought to stand in the way of progress, and opposed Jews as they were thought to do too well out of progress.

Wiseman made a name for himself as a sort of renaissance man in England, giving lectures on every subject under the sun, and providing his church with a visible presence and social acceptability. His lack of administrative tidiness led to endless troubles, but his main policy was to bring in the new devotional practices and to push forward the converts with their university background. On his death in 1865 he was succeeded by Henry Manning, a former archdeacon in the Church of England, and a man who has had a very bad press. Lytton Strachey included him in his essays on *Eminent Victorians* and his early biographies were written in the worst of possible taste, but the man himself was, despite a certain impatience, a tireless worker for good. Manning had a sense of empire, and if he felt that the Church of England was too narrow and too English for a world empire, then he saw Roman Catholicism as more suited to the task of infusing that empire with religion and using that empire to spread religion. He also, and this was unusual for the converts of his day, had a real understanding of social ills, and he did what he could to help those who suffered.

There is a tradition to the effect that Manning was insensitive to Newman, but there is a tradition that *everyone* was insensitive towards

Newman. Newman was certainly sensitive, but if his early days as a
Roman Catholic were unhappy, they were probably no more unhappy
than his days as an Anglican. The truth of the matter was that nobody
knew what to do with him. He was not a man for the rough and tumble
of parish life, and he would have been disastrous as a bishop. For some
years he was sidetracked into the post of rector of a Catholic university
in Dublin, which would never have been a successful institution even
had Newman given it more of his time. He was not permitted to live in
Oxford lest he should encourage Roman Catholics to send their sons
there, when it was church policy that they should avoid such contamina-
tion, but should go instead to an institution set up by Manning which
was an unrealistic as that of Dublin. Instead Newman presided over a
group of disciples in Birmingham, produced a literary gem in his apology
for his own life, made a topical contribution to theology in his *Grammar
of Assent*, was finally made a cardinal, and yet never fulfilled the hopes
of his admirers.

The growth of the Roman Catholic community in England was halted
in the twentieth century by the general forces of church decline, and this
has led to a massive exercise in self-examination and hand-wringing.
The suggestion has been made by more than one scholar that the whole
episode of the Second Spring was a mistake, and that the earlier, lay-
oriented, tolerant, and 'English' phase of Catholic life might have been
more appropriate. In reality it could hardly have carried Roman Catholics through the era of the Romantic Movement, and by the 1960s, when
it was being looked upon as a golden age, it was a little too remote to be
much of a model for anyone. But for the century after 1840 the times
demanded such a form of religion as English Roman Catholics so hur-
riedly and uncritically embraced. If it was not a realistic form of religion,
this was because it was, like the world, romantic. And if it did not last,
this was because no form of religion can be expected to last for ever. The
English Roman Catholics may feel that their world is collapsing, but
statistics indicate that they are doing far better than the Catholics of any
other country in Western Europe, and probably even better than those of
Ireland. That they have undergone such a frenzy of doubt and self-
analysis has only been due to the gap between the reality and their previous expectations. It is notable that the Scottish Roman Catholics, who
were so utterly indifferent to the established Church of Scotland, which
was Presbyterian and thus beyond their comprehension, had no such
high expectations through the nineteenth century and were thus un-
moved by twentieth-century decline.

5

Christmas

There are really only two possible Christian theologies. (Theologians will not like this, but theologians are not known for liking anything very much.) One theology is pessimistic about human nature and sees the critical fact of Christian activity in the Atonement, or Christ's work in saving humanity on the cross. This is in line with the teaching of St Augustine, whose low view of human nature meant that he did not really think that people could do anything at all; they could not even refuse to be saved or be damned if God wanted it. In modern times the continuation of St Augustine's teaching has been in that of John Calvin, but Calvinism, or this aspect of it, was fading in the 1830s. This could be seen in the Church of Scotland, where J. McLeod Campbell and a number of other ministers were removed from their churches for teaching that salvation was offered for all, and in America where Charles Finney had become an evangelist and found widespread acceptance for similar teaching.

The second theology is optimistic about the possibilities of human nature, and regards the critical event in Christian activity as the Incarnation, or God becoming human in Christ. This implied that humanity was capable of being accepted into the person of Christ. In its more extreme forms this optimistic theology might lead to the Pelagian heresy, which held that man could do good things even without the help of God. It would be possible to link the pessimistic strain in Christian thought to the ancient heresy of Monophysitism, which held that Christ was purely divine and scarcely human at all. It would be equally possible to link the optimistic strain to the heresy of Nestorianism, in which the human nature of Christ could exist in virtual separation from the divine nature. And on the subject of the Trinity, the pessimistic is related to the heresy of Arianism, in which Christ is not really divine, since humanity is so lowly that it cannot be allowed into the Trinity. The optimistic is related to Sabellianism in which Christ, including the human nature of Christ, is not even distinct from God the Father, who is thus almost human. But that is enough theology for our purpose. In fact it is rather more than enough.

In the 1840s there was a renewed emphasis on the Incarnation and a wide acceptance, both in Christianity and without, of the nobility of human nature. This was particularly expressed in the revival of Christmas. And, contrary to what could be assumed from modern church life, Christianity has not always made much of Christmas. It came to the fore in the early church when the Gnostics denied that Christ was human at all, and devotional aids had to teach that he was. It became prominent again in the Middle Ages when there was a threat from the Albigensians, a new kind of Gnostic, but then it fell into decline. It had little to say to the eighteenth century, and when the Evangelicals came they leaned more to the Atonement. In a volume of the *Penny Encyclopaedia* published in London in 1837, Christmas was regarded as merely a fading tradition in rural England, 'even Christmas carols are nearly gone by, and the decking of churches and of a few houses of people in humble life with holly and other evergreens, forms now almost the only indication that this great festival is at hand'. But Christmas was about to return with a rush.

It returned in various ways, not all of them religious, and one of the non-religious ways was that of Charles Dickens. He wrote his *Christmas Carol*, which was not really a carol at all but the story of Scrooge, for what Christmas trade already existed in the key year of 1843. It was an immediate success, and he later wrote a Christmas book each year and then a Christmas story in his paper, though none of these later writings is all that memorable. But even before 1843 he had published one Christmas story, and the influential Christmas chapter in his *Pickwick Papers* was published in 1836. This related the holiday visit to Old Wardle at Dingley Dell, all good food and jollity with a reversion to childhood pleasures. If the religious Christmas was the coming of the Christ Child to return us to the sinless paradise before the fall of humanity, the Dickens Christmas was a return by our own efforts to a sinless childhood. 'How many old recollections, and how many dormant sympathies, does Christmas time awaken!' gushed Dickens, and, 'Happy, happy, Christmas, that can win us back to the delusions of our childish days; that can recall to the old man the pleasures of his youth; that can transport the sailor and the traveller, thousands of miles away, back to his own fireside and his quiet home!' Something of that spirit lingers in the Christmas cards of old horse-drawn coaches, and old coaching inns, which to this day draw us back to Dingley Dell, if not to Bethlehem.

In the same spirit Dickens provided a Scrooge whose life was changed by visions of Christmas, past, present and future, but not by Christ, who does not appear in the story. Scrooge does go to church on Christmas day, but there is no note of what he did there, and his nephew's party, and his good deeds to his clerk, are much more important. Indeed, he becomes such a reformed character that in later years he is known as a man who keeps Christmas well, and what more is there to life than that? There is in the story of Scrooge, as there is in *Pickwick Papers*, though not in its specifically Christmas chapter, a strong call to philanthropy, with the well-to-do helping the worse-to-do, and this is the mark of the social reformer in Dickens. Of course this offended many of his readers, and the *Illustrated London News* of 1845 grumbled that Dickens' popularity was 'founded on portraying the amenities of life, and it will not be extended by sharpening its asperities or exaggerating its enormities'.

Yet Dickens did not understand the religious Christmas, and he did not understand that religious truths were now being expressed in a variety of cultural forms. He showed his incomprehension by writing a parody of a Royal Commission investigating the new ceremonials of the Oxford Movement, 'A vast number of witnesses being interrogated as to what they understood by the words Religion and Salvation, answered, Lighted Candles. Some said, Water, some Bread, others Little Boys; others mixed the Water, Lighted Candles, Bread and Little Boys all up together, and called the compound Faith.' Dickens was not helped by his own success in spreading the new ideas of the 1840s; if the Dickens Christmas and the Christian Christmas started with the same ideas and moved to the same conclusions, they moved on parallel tracks which never touched one another.

But there was another factor in the Christmas of the 1840s – Santa Claus. The original Saint Nicholas was supposed to have dropped dowries down chimneys or through windows to allow poor girls to marry, which legend would counter the Gnostic heretics who said that marriage was sinful. He was also supposed to have stopped a racket in which children were used for sausages, though that bit of ghoulishness appears in folklore time and again. His feast day is 6 December, and there are still supposed to be Dutch children who hang up their stockings on the night of 5 December to be filled by Santa Claus, who is, of course, Saint Nicholas in Dutch. This legend made a cultural leap from the old Dutch culture of New York to the English-speaking world in the person of Clement Clark Moore, a professor of Hebrew in a theological seminary, who wrote 'T'was the night before Christmas' in 1822 for his children, and, so the story goes, a friend sent it to the *Troy Sentinel*. That was too early in history for the poem to become popular, but there must have been stirrings of Christmas fever in America even in the 1820s, for in 1827 we find the Episcopal bishop Philander Chase writing to his wife, 'The devil has stolen from us . . . Christmas, the day of our spiritual redemption, and converted it into a day of worldly festivity, shooting and swearing.' Bishops have been saying that sort of thing ever since.

In 1844, at the height of the Christmas revival, Moore published a volume of poems including the one about Santa Claus, which made that gentleman famous, and probably made Moore the most influential biblical scholar of modern times. Stockings were soon hung by fireplaces throughout the English-speaking world, and then throughout the non-English-speaking world, and families were listening to the poem on Christmas Eve as if it were Holy Writ. In due course the poem itself became less popular, and it really is no treasure of English verse, while the miniature Santa became full-size, and dressed in red, and a symbol of generosity, and even generosity to those in need. Of course the anthropologist cannot view Santa Claus, round and red, carried through the winter skies in a chariot drawn by mythological beasts, entering houses by the chimney and leaving a gift by a fireplace which can only be linked to the gift of fire, without identifying him with the old sun-god, but that sun-god had come to be identified with Christ, so the thing had come full circle.

There were other marks of Christmas coming back to life in that era. The first Christmas card in England was printed in 1843 and showed a family at Christmas dinner with a verse about helping one's poorer neighbours. Christmas carols had been collected in the west of England as early as 1822, just before they were expected to perish completely, and in 1833 a book of them had been published for actual use, with the title, *Christmas Carols: Ancient and Modern*, which title was later used for a complete hymn book. In Germany the Christmas tree, actually a small shrub, had become popular around 1800, replacing the pyramid of candles which used up grease from slaughtered livestock. The custom was to slaughter livestock in December when forage was running low, and when the weather was cold enough for the resultant meat not to rot away, and this is the origin of much of our Christmas fare today. It meant tallow for candles, and mince for pies, and plum puddings, and the goose of Christmas which had been fattened on stubble.

There has always been a certain tension between the Christian Christmas and the Dickens Christmas, but both are rooted in a high view of humanity and a high view of the creation. If the main thing in the Christian religion is that God uses human nature to save his people and his world, then human nature is important and, despite its fall, it is good. Whether we see its goodness in humanity as created by God before the fall of mankind, or existing in childhood to this day, will seem rather a small matter to the average observer of Christmas. But it is clear that a doctrine of the goodness of human nature will have tremendous consequences for art, education, literature, politics, and almost everything else. Here it will be enough to attempt to sketch the different traditions of the two Christmases in politics, while not attempting to answer the main question. That question is whether the Dickens Christmas and the Santa Claus Christmas are ultimately dependent on the Christmas of the Christ Child at Bethlehem, and will fade away without it, or whether the new stress on Incarnation in the churches was part of a wider change of cultural climate teaching the goodness of mankind. It may be that both answers are ultimately correct.

But to consider politics, there can be no doubt that the 1840s were years of political upheaval. In England there was Chartism, and 1848 has come to be identified with popular revolutions almost everywhere in Europe. But along with this there was a specific tradition of what was later called Christian socialism, mainly Anglican and harking back to a supposed mediaeval society in which everyone was happy and went to church and then danced around a maypole. This mediaeval Christmas and mediaeval political system was dominant in English thought; in Scotland there was an almost complete lack of a mediaeval Christmas, and instead an acceptance of the Dickens idea of the natural nobility of mankind, leading to a Christian socialism which was hardly Christian at all – or was only Christian in the sense of the Sermon on the Mount.

It is easy to make fun of this type of Christian socialism. A recent author, Callum Brown, has written convincingly that, 'From the outset, Christian socialism displaced religious objectives and assisted rather than stemmed the secularization of social policy.' If some Christians hoped that their work to improve social conditions was going to bring people to Christianity, they were wrong, but they should have known they were wrong. And they had no choice; if they could improve social conditions it was their duty to do so, even if this undermined the idea that better social conditions could only come from widespread acceptance of Christianity. The truth is that people become Christian for religious reasons and not for political reasons, and if the belief that they can be lured into Christianity in their search for social justice is going to be destroyed, so much the better.

Of course much of the socialist message now seems ludicrous. The Socialist Sunday Schools which taught pure ethics, having outgrown dogma, are now dead. They died of dullness. The simple faith that most people were good and decent and would do the right thing if artificial restraints were removed, and children were given singing and dancing and flower-drill, has hardly outlasted such people as Tolstoy or Thomas Hardy. The idea that all questions could be solved by getting everyone to sit down at the table has never recovered from the appeasement of Hitler at Munich in 1938. There is still a lingering idea that primitive peoples are better than industrial peoples, and holiday-makers from industrial nations still think they can soak up goodness in the landscape and alongside the culture of those untainted by factory life. But this raises the question of race.

In trying to preach the goodness of humanity in a world where human beings do evil, it is tempting to solve the problem by excluding some human beings from humanity. This is probably not the origin of modern racism, but it has certainly helped racism along. If Western thinkers considered Africans to be barbarous, they could be relegated to some semi-human category, living in some assumed state of the unconscious, or slowly developing to fuller humanity. And the same could be done with women, who were credited with all sorts of characteristics which men were assumed not to possess, until men and women were virtually separate species. Of course non-Europeans were inevitably caught up in this process, and finding it useless and perhaps distasteful to make themselves equal with Europeans, claimed to have all sorts of desirable characteristics which Europeans did not have. These were musical sensitivity, compassion, intuitive understanding, and other things which gave them status but which were not much use in balancing the national budget. Similarly women claimed feminine characteristics, usually the same as non-Europeans, and virtually wrote themselves out of the human race, which was an understandable aim in view of what had been done to them by the dominant gender in that race. Much of the argument over the ordination of women has hinged on the question of whether men and women were the same species or not.

Finally, a summary of modern politics might be that the left believes in the goodness of humanity, and the right does not. The left can thus believe that all will go well as soon as the unnatural work of some vicious elite is detected and removed. On the other hand, the right believes that humanity is fundamentally bad and can only be forced to work through the application of sticks and carrots, though the right also believes in an elite – the governing group which will ensure the existence of sticks and carrots to direct the worst instincts of the masses into profitable activity. But like all summaries this is dangerously misleading and incomplete; we cannot assume that left-wingers are enthusiastic about Christmas, and right-wingers about Good Friday. But we should be aware of the importance of the argument about the goodness or wickedness of humanity, and we should be aware that there is more to Christmas than Dingley Dell or Santa Claus.

6

Methodism and the Social Sciences

There are dark corners to the study of Methodism. This is not just because some of the major questions are unanswered, and perhaps can never be answered. It is because the waters have been muddied by the boots of social scientists. The result is that there are almost as many theories of Methodism as there are Methodists.

Eli Halevy was a distinguished French historian who wrote of the history of England. He noted, as any Frenchman would, that England had no French Revolution. This remarkable fact had to be explained. What did England have in the eighteenth century which France did not? The answer was obvious. Methodism. The Methodists had given English workers and peasants an ideology which led them to work and not to agitate, and their religious hopes had made them indifferent to social and economic complaints. In justice to Halevy, it must be admitted that there was more to it than this. Halevy also believed that the English were a serious race, while the French were not, but if the English seriousness led to Methodism, then Methodism could still be the factor which prevented the English revolution. Today the Halevy thesis is out of fashion, but it still reappears in modern forms. Perhaps the most appealing of these argues that Methodism blurred the distinction between Dissent and the Church of England, since it had a foot in each camp, and thus rising Dissenters could join the Church of England by using Methodism as a transit lounge. In fact anyone who wanted to join the Church of England could do so without using Methodism, since the Church of England ran the whole range of social classes and was probably stronger than other religious bodies in the lowest. Furthermore, if the upper layers of society were closed to Dissenters, they were also closed to most Anglicans. There may have been some way in which Methodism aided social mobility, but if so then nobody really knows what it was. However, the main lesson to be learned from this is that religious bodies are, surprisingly, religious. If they are studied as social or economic bodies the result is confusion, even though there is a social and an economic aspect to any religious body.

If Methodists once took pride in having saved England from the guillotine, in due course they were blamed for having condemned millions to factory slavery. This blame is particularly heaped upon them by E. P. Thompson, an entrancing writer, who has a theory that mill-owners welcomed Methodism (in fact most distrusted Methodism) because it gave their workers a 'moral machinery'. These words come from a book, *The Philosophy of Manufacturing*, by Andrew Ure. He argued that manufacturers should treat their workers well not only in matters physical but also in matters spiritual. The manufacturers would thus provide the moral machinery to make the workers, in Thompson's words, their own slave-drivers. In fact Ure seems to have been a phil-anthropist trying to wheedle mill-owners into good works by any means possible, but misunderstanding Ure can never be counted a sin. The whole notion of 'moral machinery' rests upon a psychological theory of the human person being a blank page on which anyone can write, and this is a theory which recurs again and again. Ure's writing did, how-ever, help Thompson to rail against the 'psychological atrocities of the Sunday school' in which innocent children were scarred for life by fear of hell and slaved away in factories to avoid that fate. But what is unfor-tunate about all this is that it obscures the parts of the argument which really do make sense. Where conditions were appalling people may well have looked elsewhere in despair, though there is a good deal of evidence that the followers of other-worldly religion were not the poorest but those who had achieved a certain security. And people newly arrived in the cities did need work-discipline, and did get this from the Sunday schools, though the Sunday schools were usually working-class institu-tions supplying the children of the workers with just those ideals which workers themselves valued.

We are on different ground with the Weber thesis, though the ground is equally soggy. And the Weber thesis is actually much older than Weber himself, who was a founder of sociology. As early as 1832 Thomas Chalmers, the Scottish churchman, was comparing Protestant and Catholic cantons in Switzerland to show that the Protestants did better because of their religion, though he did not work the theory out in detail. In 1862 a Brazilian named Tavares Bastos wanted Protestant immigra-tion to that country because Protestants would benefit the economy. In

1875 the Belgian economist Victor de Laveleya argued that it was religion not race which determined the economic advance of a nation, and Protestant Germans would always surpass Catholic Latins in the creation of wealth. As for Max Weber, he wrote his book at the beginning of this century, very much off the top of his head, and perhaps not at the top of his form. But if the Weber theory is to be rejected, it should be noted that Weber only accepted what was accepted by everyone else, and made an honest effort to explain it. If he did not succeed, neither did anyone else.

Weber's *Protestant Ethic and the Spirit of Capitalism* held that Protestants succeeded in business because they had a calling. Furthermore, this was an individual calling, as Protestants were disenchanted with the world and thus with the communities in which they lived. Again, the doctrine of election to salvation as taught by Calvin meant that Calvinists had to work their heads off to show they were amongst the elect, since the elect would do better than others in this world. And since Calvinists were dissuaded from spending their profits on idle luxury, they had to re-invest it, and this made the economy thrive. The whole thing might be summed up in Weber's phrase, 'a good conscience in money-lending'. Of course this theory flattered Protestants in the days when money-making was highly regarded, and there were the inevitable Catholic attempts to prove that it was really Catholicism which had given capitalism to a grateful world.

It was all very exciting, and it turned the tables on the Marxists, who claimed that all religion was only a pale reflection of economic reality. Here, at long last, was absolute proof that economic activity was controlled by religion! But in due course the Weber thesis lost its charm. It was remembered that the earliest states to undergo industrial development were not so much united in religious outlook as united in having coal, iron and waterpower. Yet there is one thing which does remain of Weber's theory. He may have had a distorted view of what Calvinism was all about, and he may have applied denominational labels to nations without due care, but when he said that basic beliefs influenced behaviour and thus economics, he was saying something which cannot be denied. Religious beliefs may not have been the only or even the main factors as work, but they were factors at work. And in making this point Weber may have said something which would otherwise have been forgotten in his day. Yet the details of the Weber thesis cannot be sustained, nor can the details of any of the other social and economic theories which held religion to dominate society and economics or, on the other hand, to be dominated by them. This means that we are forced to regard Methodism as a religious movement. This would have horrified our forefathers, but new ideas always horrify somebody.

This does not explain why it arose. It does not explain why it flourished in some areas but not in others. If we must find a reason for the thing, then it may be in Wesley's appeal to 'the law and the testimony', rather than to the light of reason alone, or to the light of reason plus something a little less clear. Even at the height of the Deist threat there were whole sections of English society in which nobody knew about Deism and nobody cared. They could well have been tired of a theology which was intended to counter a threat which they did not know, and the more positive preaching of Wesley might have been welcomed.

But there is more than this. John Wesley was a ferocious opponent of Calvinism, though it is not considered polite to mention this today. If Calvinism has a low estimate of humanity and what it can do, and what can be done with it, Wesley said anyone could be saved and some could even achieve total sanctification. In an age when man was considered to be the most supreme being around, the Calvinists reacted by saying that man was really pretty bad and would generally come to a bad end, and at best would not come to a particularly good one. Wesley rejected the spirit of the age in most things, but within the limits of Evangelical orthodoxy he was nearer to his age than the Calvinists, and this may have made his form of Christianity available to those who would never have gone over to the Calvinists. Yet it may be that the whole question of why Methodism came to exist cannot be answered and should not be asked. The big questions have no answers, and that is as it should be.

If the beginnings of Methodism are puzzling, it is a relief to move on to matters more certain. And the later history of Methodism is more certain; it could not be less certain. John Wesley died in 1791 leaving power in the hands of the 'Legal Hundred' preachers of his movement, and with the future of Methodism unresolved. After various shifts it was decided in 1795 that preachers could administer the Lord's Supper for Methodists, though there was to be no ordination. Thus did the Wesleyan movement become a church. Calvinistic Methodists in Wales went their own way, eventually taking the title 'Presbyterian'. In 1810 the Primitive Methodists, going back to the early forms of the movement, separated from Wesleyan Methodism and began a long history of lively dissent. But the major body was still the Wesleyan Methodist, and this was constitutionally weak and easily dominated. It came to be dominated by one Jabez Bunting.

Jabez Bunting belonged to the most despised group in church history. He was an administrator. He had no public personality and even today many things about him are a mystery. The son of a radical tailor, he became a Methodist minister with a special interest in missionary affairs. Nonetheless, he had no desire to be a missionary hmiself, and he distrusted evangelism as it admitted untrustworthy elements into the church. In 1803 Bunting began a campaign against the venerable Thomas Coke, who had let the Missionary Committee get into a muddle. But Coke fought back and had Bunting exiled to the provinces, and it took him ten years to fight his way back. After founding a popular missionary society in Leeds, Bunting became Conference Secretary in 1814. Since the Legal Hundred were the senior ministers they included many who were senile, and there was much support for Bunting when he proposed a change. He arranged that every fourth vacancy should be filled by election from those with fourteen years of service; by pure coincidence he himself had fourteen years of service. In due course he was not only Conference Secretary but dominated the Missionary Committee, the Theological Institution, the Book Room, the church press, and the Stationing Committee which had sent him out to grass in Coke's day. He could now exile his enemies to the wilderness, and he could reward his supporters.

But if Bunting was such a monster of depravity, we might ask why Methodism tolerated him. The answer is that he gave many Methodists what they wanted. He gave them social respectability by appearing on political platforms with Tory leaders, at a time when Methodists were still regarded as ignorant ranters and political levellers. He now made Methodists honorary members of the establishment. But that was not all. He brought to Methodism the high church ways of all religious bodies in the 1840s, and these ways had deep roots in Wesley's sacramentalism. Ordination was introduced in 1836. There was some talk of apostolic succession. There was also talk of the 'brutal ignorance' of the uneducated laity. Methodism was moving closer to the Church of England.

Yet reaction was inevitable. Behind the programme of Methodism, which brought respectability and a renewed buoyancy in the Pension Fund, there was not much of the reality of the Gothic Revival. Jabez Bunting may have been sincere in his devotion, but he produced little consciousness of the church as a real community. It was far more an apparatus for restraining brutal ignorance. As for the idea of a church separate from the state, Bunting had brought it closer to the state, though any form of state recognition could never be much of a threat, Bunting's programme looked like jobbery and ultimately it was jobbery. And Methodists saw this.

The result was the scandal of the Fly Sheets, which attacked Bunting and his Book Room clique from 1844 until nearly the end of the decade. The Fly Sheets were scarcely edifying in tone, but the 'reformers' in Methodism managed to elect one of theirs as President of Conference in 1845. However, this did not seriously undermine the Bunting influence, and Bunting demanded that every member of Conference should take an oath not to have been the author of the Fly Sheets and not to know who had been. One man refused to take the oath and was expelled by the votes of all but two, who were then expelled in turn. As we read of this extraordinary procedure, it is ironic to discover secular historians telling us that democracy in England owed so much to the example of and training in Methodism. That claim, though vastly exaggerated, may just have a glimmer of truth behind it, yet it is not supported by the story of the Fly Sheets. Large numbers of people were lost to Methodism before the agitation died down, and control of chapels in some parts of the country were contested by one group or another not only with rhetoric but even with blunderbusses. Methodism was never again to embrace as large a proportion of the population as it did before 1849.

Yet the centre held until the aged Bunting died. And something of his church policy remained in Wesleyan Methodism. The reformers who left formed new bodies which came together as the United Methodists of later days, while there were still the Primitive Methodists as an alternative. It was as if the Tractarian high churchmen of the Church of England had been able to expel everyone else, which would not have worried some of them had they been in a position to manage it. Again, the relationship of Wesleyan, Primitive and United Methodists was strikingly similar to that of the Church of Scotland, the Free Church, and the United Presbyterians north of the border, both in relative strength and in theological emphasis. And as those three bodies united in Scotland in 1929, so did the three wings of English Methodism unite in 1930. It is tempting to suggest that Wesley's movement had come back to unity after two centuries, and yet Methodism has been and perhaps always shall be of many hues and different emphases.

7

Scotland

Very early in the eighteenth century somebody in Scotland found an old book in an abandoned cottage and modern Scottish church life began. The book was *The Marrow of Modern Divinity* and it was an English work from Cromwell's time. It was and is almost unreadable. However, it was important since it got right away from the idea of a God who shows his benevolence in creation, and it also got away from the idea of 'limited atonement'. Limited atonement was the doctrine that God selected some for salvation, and others for damnation, and this approach was linked to the name of Calvin, who may or may not have intended this much. It is impossible to be too definite about this, but limited atonement may have been a seventeenth-century reaction against the optimism of the Reformation age, though in the eighteenth century it may have been used as a counter-balance to the universal application of God's grace through creation, spread flat like wallpaper. The *Marrow* was duly republished in Edinburgh in 1719, and condemned by the General Assembly of the Church of Scotland in the following year; Calvinism was to remain dominant in Scottish Presbyterianism until it began to crack in the 1830s. Yet the *Marrow* was to form the mindset of the Seceders who were virtually put out of the Church of Scotland in 1733, and who led to a variety of small denominations, most of which joined together in the United Presbyterian Church in 1847. Had they been English they might have become Methodist, but they might not. Their importance is in showing that Calvinism was not going to maintain a monopoly in Scottish religion, and that a broader Evangelicalism was possible.

In the year 1712 the new all-British Parliament passed an act to give toleration to Episcopalians in Scotland who conformed to the successors of William of Orange instead of to the Stuarts. The motive for this act is still obscure, as are so many other things in Scottish church history, but it was probably a desperate and ill-advised attempt to buy off Episcopalians who, with their bishops, had refused to desert the Stuart monarchy in 1688. Instead they had gone off into the wilderness from which they would support rebellions in 1715 and 1745. This act was resented by the new Presbyterian establishment, and was probably contrary to the Act of Union of 1707, but it had a secondary clause which re-instituted patronage or the right of landowners to nominate ministers to particular parishes in the Church of Scotland. At first this made little difference as there was a shortage of ministers, the Episcopalians having been put out, and parishes were glad to get anybody at all. But by the time of the Seceders patronage was unpopular with many, and it was on this issue that the Secession actually occurred, though theology lay behind it. And patronage was to break up the Church of Scotland.

To understand this it must first be stated that church parties in England and Scotland were very different. In Scotland there were 'moderates': the descendants of those who had proved that God was benevolent. Such people had died out in England. In England there was the High Church party, stressing the independence of the church, and there was the Low Church party, which was Evangelical. But in Scotland the Evangelical party stood for the independence of the church, and was thus a High Church party as well. This situation was seen in 1799 when certain Evangelicals tried to replace the Kirk with a network of Congregational chapels, and were condemned by the General Assembly in a 'Pastoral Admonition' which won the support of most Evangelicals. And from 1833 the Evangelicals dominated the General Assembly, replacing the moderate leadership.

The Evangelical leader was Thomas Chalmers, minister of Kilmany in Fife, lecturer in chemistry and writer on political economy and astronomy and just about everything else. He had been converted to Evangelicalism in 1809 and later served in Glasgow parishes before becoming a professor in St Andrews, of moral philosophy which he also happened to know, and later at Edinburgh, of divinity. He also invented a new way of washing his hands but, alas, that perished with him.

But Chalmers was faced with an irresistible force meeting an immovable object. Political theory was turning to doctrines of the absolute sovereignty of the state; this theory was seen in the writings of John Austin, who looked at the Act of Union of 1707 which promised to preserve the rights of the Church of Scotland. He said that while it might be good advice, it could never bind a sovereign parliament which had every right to abolish not only the Church of Scotland but also, if it chose, the Church of England. On the other hand, all churches in the 1840s were stressing their divine foundation and their spiritual independence of the state, and this was leading to collisions between churches and states in Germany, France, Italy, South America, Ireland, England, and of course Scotland. To begin with, Chalmers insisted that the establishment of the Church of Scotland by the state did not mean that the state could put any man into a Scottish pulpit, nor did he oppose patronage in theory. But the Evangelicals hoped to make it conform to modern doctrines of the church by having the congregation's 'call' to the man nominated by the patron in each parish be no longer a mere formality, but rather a necessary part of the process. However, their way of doing so was inept. In 1834 the General Assembly passed a 'Veto Act' whereby the people could veto a patron's nomination; it is only fair to say they sought legal advice before doing this. Yet the Veto Act was not clearly in accordance with church law, as it had not been approved by presbyteries, and it had a fatal flaw. When a man was nominated by a patron he had civil rights which were threatened by the veto, and if a probationer had waited for years till presented by a patron, often assisting an aged minister or teaching school until his time came, he was unlikely to take his rejection lightly. It was to be noted that patrons did not go to law against the Veto Act; they seldom had much interest in who was to minister in parishes in which the great landowners no longer lived, and they usually sought to satisfy the people. Furthermore, the vast majority of nominations did satisfy the people. In only a handful of parishes did the matter go to law, and of the parishes concerned one is well-known as it is near a major golf-course, but the others are near nothing at all. The question of the Veto Act was not a question of everyday concern but a matter of principle. Finally, the patron could not nominate anyone he liked. He was limited to men already ordained in other parishes, or men licensed as probationers by a presbytery which had thus accepted that they were fit to be ordained. The church chose ministers; the patron could only choose which minister served in a particular parish.

The legal wrangles began with Archterarder. A nominee had been vetoed by the people in 1834 and had then gone to court on the advice of a legal luminary named John Hope. Scotland's Court of Session not only ordered him to be given the salary and use of the manse, but ordered that he be ordained, which was a spiritual matter and not a civil one. It was to be many years before he was ordained, and he then proved to be an excellent minister, but by that time those who opposed him had left the Church of Scotland anyway. In Lethendy in 1833 the court tried to put in a nominee of the Crown who had been vetoed, even though the Crown accepted the Veto Act and nominated someone else. The presbytery ignored the court and ordained the second nominee, and was subjected to 'solemn censure' by the court. At Marnoch in 1837 a former assistant to the minister was nominated by the patron, vetoed by the people, and then ordained by the Presbytery of Strathbogie at the command of the Court of Session but despite the prohibition of the General Assembly. Virtually the entire congregation walked out of the ordination service, and the seven ministers involved were suspended by the church. In 1841 at Culsalmond the people vetoed a nomination but the Presbytery of Garioch ordained the man anyway, though in the manse rather than the church as there was a 'riot' going on in the church. The new minister was promptly suspended by the church, and at this point the Court of Session drew back and did not intervene.

It was hoped that wiser counsels would prevail in both church and state. Lord Aberdeen tried to get Thomas Chalmers to agree to a parliamentary bill which would give the church the liberty it needed, but the details were tricky. By law a reason for rejection had to be given, and Aberdeen asserted that this need not be a major reason – a man could be rejected for having red hair. But Aberdeen had allowed John Hope to become his adviser, and Hope wanted no compromise. It was said that Hope wept when the Church of Scotland finally split in 1843, and he has been known to history as 'Crocodile Hope', but a recent chronicler of his underground burrowings has called him the 'mole'. Yet even without Hope the result would probably have been the same.

However, the courts were now troubling the Church of Scotland in matters other than patronage. Ministers deposed for fraud or immorality were claiming protection from the civil courts, though in fact they got very little from those courts. Two hundred ministers of newly created parishes were declared not to be parish ministers and thus not entitled to be represented in the General Assembly. A group of Seceder ministers who had rejoined the Church of Scotland in 1839 had been given parish boundaries, and now these were declared to be invalid. The situation was becoming intolerable, and it was becoming a national issue, with Chalmers saying that spiritual independence was 'the peculiar glory of the Church of Scotland'. That the Church of England was going through a similar experience was ignored; the English were supposed to like having their religion dictated to them by the state.

When the General Assembly of 1843 met in Edinburgh its Evangelical majority had slipped away for the first time in a decade. The outgoing and Evangelical moderator spoke of the need to separate, and three abreast ministers and elders walked out and down the street to another hall where they convened the first General Assembly of the Free Church of Scotland. Of the former ministers, 451 had left to join the new body, while 752 stayed where they were. And with vigour and generosity the laity set about finding stipends, building churches, and making the Free Church a resounding success. But what nobody could have predicted was that the 'Auld Kirk', instead of being the empty shell left by the Free Churchmen, also flourished. And for Free Churchmen that was perhaps the unkindest cut of all.

It may be asked if the Disruption of the Church of Scotland in 1843 was a good thing, and the answer must be that it was not. It might have been avoided by a bit of muddling around the principles until passions had died. 1843 was the high point of the Gothic Revival and 'spiritual independence' fervour in general, and a few years later the atmosphere might have been calmer and solutions more acceptable. But faced as they were by the improper demands of the courts, those who walked out of the church cannot be faulted for responding as they did.

Once the Disruption had occurred, there were three main churches in Scottish Presbyterianism. The Church of Scotland or 'Auld Kirk' was the most widespread and least Evangelical; in 1868 it had 422,000 communicants. The Free Church had 250,000 in the same year; it was Evangelical and conservative in doctrine. The United Presbyterians had 160,000 and tended to liberalism in both theology and politics. And after 1843 no group increased its percentage of the population at the expense of any other, until the last quarter of the century when the Church of Scotland began to pull ahead, just as did the Church of England south of the border. But what was common to all Scottish churches was their weakened allegiance to the 'limited atonement', or Calvin's doctrine of election by God to either salvation or damnation.

In fact, the real change had occurred in the 1830s. Thomas Erskine, an Episcopal layman, had written a series of books against election, though modern readers will be hard pressed to know what he was saying. And some Church of Scotland ministers began to preach unlimited atonement and to pay for their daring; John McLeod Campbell was deposed in 1831, and later wrote a book on the salvation of mankind by Christ which is still read today. Four other ministers were deposed in the following years, yet if they were cast out, their ideas were not. They had been concerned with the Incarnation, the dwelling of God in human flesh and later in the church, and the love of God rather than the power of God soon came to be dominant in Scottish preaching even if Calvinism was never formally put aside. In 1873 Moody floated in from America and had the greatest success of his life when Scots responded to his preaching of God's love for all; this had probably been the actual faith of the Scottish churches for decades before they realized that it was so. The theological formularies had to make way for this development. The United Presbyterians were embarrassed by having to try ministers for rejecting election as set forth in the Westminster Confession when nobody actually believed it any more, and in 1879 they provided it with a framework, calling it 'necessarily imperfect'. Unfortunately they then made a doctrine of collecting money for missions, though they did not go so far as to state that this must be in little envelopes bearing dates. The Church of Scotland gingerly changed the way in which elders swore to the Confession, while in 1892 the Free Church produced a Declaratory Act describing how they held the Westminster Confession, which in this case meant not teaching predestination. This was a fine document, but it did not convince all of those in the Highlands where theological development had been on different lines from that in Lowland Scotland. A small group seceded in 1893, to form the Free Presbyterian Church.

In worship there was surprisingly little change, and most of what there was occurred in the addition of hymns. The sacrament of the Lord's Supper ceased to be received at special tables; these were replaced by a small communion table, while the people remained in their pews. Obviously the sacrament must have been seen in a different light once it was distanced from the people in this way, but although it was probably much the same experience as other churches underwent in the Gothic revival, in Scotland the change took a century to achieve and was not the subject of much notice or dissent. Biblical criticism was also introduced with surprisingly little dissent, though an Aberdeen professor of the Free Church, W. Robertson Smith, attracted attention by writing successive articles for the *Encyclopaedia Britannica* in which he set forth the latest German findings. The volume in which he wrote on 'Angels' went unnoticed, but that on 'Bible' led to a trial by the General Assembly and Robertson Smith was let off with a caution. Then came the volume with an article on 'Hebrew Language and Literature', and in 1881 he was removed from his post, though allowed to remain as a minister. This was illogical; nobody thought that he had corrupted his students, and they were really afraid of what he would do to the laity. He went off to Cambridge and was never heard of again. But even at the proceedings which condemned him, those who taught biblical criticism in other colleges publicly claimed their right to do so, and through exhaustion or dawning understanding nobody tried to stop them.

If the first great achievement of the Church of Scotland in the modern age had been to divide, the next great achievement was to undo the first. The Free Church and the United Presbyterians began talking in the 1850s, but by the time things came to a vote in 1867, over a quarter of those in the Free Church General Assembly were opposed, so union was postponed. The opposition came overwhemingly from the Highlands, where a form of church-state co-operation still worked at the local level, so that Highlanders favoured establishment and feared union with United Presbyterians who were strict 'voluntarists' or opponents of any form of state connection. Yet the Highlanders were generally Calvinist, and their strict interpretation of the sovereignty of God meant that he had to be seen to be Lord of nations as well as Lord of saints, so establishment, however theoretical, was vital to their faith.

The next step was for both Free Church and United Presbyterians to campaign for the disestablishment of the Church of Scotland, which was also to be stripped of its financial endowments. This was a strange business; injuring a church as a means by which to unite with it. But those were the years in which free choice mattered most, and one church having more status and money than another was seen as hindering free choice amongst possible churchgoers. In effect, it was considered to be a conspiracy in restraint of free trade. Furthermore, the Church of Scotland had abolished patronage in 1874, which Free Churchmen had only achieved by going out into the wilderness, and they objected to the Kirk getting such freedom at no cost at all. They also suspected that the real intention was to win over Free Churchmen now that a barrier had been removed. But disestablishment depended on Gladstone, who was aware that demand for such a step was very limited, and did nothing in his usual careful way. The campaign only made people believe that if a church had in any way changed its nature then it should lose its property, and this was to hurt the Free Church in the future. And, once again, the Highlanders were antagonized.

Nonetheless, a renewed attempt merged the Free Church and the United Presbyterians in 1900. In the Free General Assembly it passed by 486 votes to 38, but the defeated minority went through all the courts, and in 1904 the House of Lords gave all the property of the former Free Church to a handful in the Highlands. The reason, broadly speaking, was that 'when men subscribe money for a particular object, and leave it behind them for the promition of that object, their successors have no right to change the object endowed'. Specifically, it was held that the Free Church had abandoned belief in the principle of establishment, which was still acclaimed by Chalmers in 1843, in order to meet the beliefs of the United Presbyterians, and there was a complaint that they had also abandoned Calvinism, though since the dissidents had already swallowed that action in 1892, this was a very much weaker argument. In past years it used to be held that the judges were mainly English and did not understand Scottish views on spiritual independence, but modern observers are not so harsh on the judges. The decision may have been nonsense, but it was probably good law. Perhaps the decision would have gone the other way had it been argued by the lawyers for the United Free Church, as the merged body called itself, that establishment was not a basic belief of the old Free Church, instead of arguing that a church could do as it wanted anyway. However, the result was intolerable, since the Highland group could not use all the property, and their attempt to do so showed how little support they actually had. Two years later an act of Parliament divided the property between the United Free Church and the remaining Free Church according to numbers. Probably there should have been such an act in the first place, but it went against the grain for some Free Churchmen to admit that they needed it.

The next step was reunion between the United Free Church and the Church of Scotland. There was nothing to divide them except their attitude to the state, and the Church of Scotland managed to have establishment of religion changed to recognition of religion, while the same 1906 act which had sorted out the United Free Church union had also given the Church of Scotland freedom to change all but its most fundamental beliefs. That only left endowments. These, called 'teinds', were tied up with harvests, and landowners paid variable sums to their ministers each year. It was agreed that these endowments, which in fact only gave the Kirk a small proportion of its income, were church and not state property, and should be kept by the church, though no longer under control of the special Court of Teinds. This was done in an act of Parliament in 1925, and the way was now clear for the union of 1929, which included all members of the Church of Scotland, though a few of the United Free Church continued independently.

Modern Scottish church history is sometimes presented as if it had taken place on some other planet. In fact the major events are almost exactly duplicated in overseas Presbyterianism, and not just from loyalty to a Scottish homeland. They are also paralleled in English Methodism, and to a lesser extent in the Church of England. Scottish church history may thus be described as a particularly Scottish reaction to the same forces which occurred elsewhere, with much the same results as were found elsewhere. Scotland may be distinctive, but it is still part of a larger story.

8

Ireland

It has sometimes been suggested that Irish history is a treacherous bog, and if this is an exaggeration, it is still true to say that Irish church history is very treacherous indeed, with dark patches to swallow the unwary.

One problem is that the Irish outside Ireland have created the picture of Ireland held by most outsiders and not a few insiders. The fact of emigration cannot be ignored, though it can be misunderstood and is misunderstood. Of course without the potato from the New World most of the Irish population would not have been there to emigrate, so there is good reason to consider the emigration a homecoming, but Ireland is not unusual in having been dependent on an overseas crop.

Another problem is the Irish cast of mind. The Irish have an unfortunate habit of taking ideas at their face value. The Scots weigh them against experience, and the English do not have them at all, but the Irish keep them in all purity and then unexpectedly act upon them. This worries other people who think that it is not good form. They say it must be because the Irish are Celtic. In fact the Irish are the usual mixture of various strains of races, much like England or Scotland, though with somewhat less Anglo-Saxon contribution.

Irish history is considered to be tragic, because that was the thing to be in the age of Gothic romanticism. Yet few small nations have done so well, and many large nations have done much worse. Apart from the horrors of famine, Ireland managed to export its surplus population in a fairly orderly way and they went to areas where they have prospered. Even the Civil War of 1920 was a tame affair by European standards; brutality was kept in check by a somewhat pedantic legality. For the Irish have always been law-abiding; their problem has been deciding with which law they should abide. Through modern history their crime

rates have always been remarkably low, and their sobriety high in comparison with nations such as Scotland. Their demand for home rule has
been a very modest demand, and their loyalty to the crown embarrass-
ingly steady until very near the end. Nor have they been religious bigots.
Until about 1820 Catholics and Protestants generally got along well, and
wished each other well. The change came in two ways. First, the new
ideas of nineteenth-century romanticism made churches important, and
a plurality of churches intolerable. Secondly, the quantum leap from the
old eighteenth-century mental world to the new nineteenth-century
world was taken unevenly. The Catholics got one foot on each side of
the stream; the Protestants stood firmly in the middle. Nothing was to
distinguish the two sides more than the Protestant emphasis on contract
law, on agreements made and for ever binding, and on ideas totally
forgotten in Britain, while Catholics could be romantic and sad and
generally Gothic on the one hand, but on the other hand just as constitutionally minded and legalistic and republican (in the philosophical sense)
as the Protestants. Had the Catholics not had this legalistic side, they
would not have understood the ideas of the Protestants sufficiently well
to reject them. For, in the end, all Irish have more in common with one
another than with anyone else. The Irish think more. They may not
think better, but they think more.

We begin with the Protestants, which in Irish terminology means
Church of Ireland only; these are Episcopalians or Anglicans, though
there is lingering dislike of the latter term. Of events in their history we
are warned that 'it is important not to view them as a logical narrative'.
Could they ever have succeeded in being other than they were? Why
did they not? There is no answer. It is by no means clear why sixteenth-
century Ireland went the way it did, and some historians have even
argued that the matter was not really determined until the nineteenth
century. That is probably going too far, but there were clearly a multi-
tude of Irish around 1800 who were not committed to anything more
than a vaguely Christian set of values. When they did become committed, it was to a renewed Roman Catholicism which enthusiastically
accepted the Gothic revival as the Church of Ireland did not. Perhaps
the Church of Ireland had too tight a structure to permit change; perhaps it was worried about Unitarianism, which always lay beneath the
soil of Ireland, or was thought to do so; or perhaps there was some other
factor, but it continued into the nineteenth century with the face of the
eighteenth. And when it was taken over by a late Evangelicalism, the
lines were already drawn across Ireland and decisions already made.

It was only mildly influenced by the high church doctrines of the 1840s, and since these could not find a place beside an Evangelicalism still young and vigorous, they did not so much change the Church of Ireland as leave it completely. The Brethren movement was to be the equivalent in Ireland of Anglo-Catholicism in England.

The Church of Ireland had two obvious weaknesses. First it was supported by tithes or ground-rents extracted from a mainly Roman Catholic population. In earlier days this was not seen as such an injustice as it was later, but in the nineteenth century it became intolerable. Second, the Church of Ireland served as a convenient source of dignified posts for English clergymen, perhaps pious enough in themselves, whose families had influence with government. As such things became less tolerable in England they became less tolerable in Ireland.

In 1833 the British government suppressed ten Irish bishoprics to spread their revenues more usefully around the church. This was undoubtedly right, but should governments do this? At that time nobody else could, but the precedent worried not only high churchmen in England but even Cardinal Antonelli in Rome, who was against disestablishment or state interference with church revenues anywhere. And in 1869 an act was passed totally to disestablish the Church of Ireland two years later, giving freedom to allow it (to its own surprise as much as everyone else's) to grow stronger, not weaker. The dominant Evangelicalism became official, and the church became more Irish as local men filled bishoprics and deaneries, with local money paying the bills. But there was no growth; it was too late for anyone to be uncommitted and thus recruited, and emigration effected Protestants more than it did Catholics. Yet the Church of Ireland proved very successful at resisting English ways, and was to export its own type of Anglicanism alongside that of England. This Irish type had a specially old-fashioned concern for the creation, and its organization was as constitutional as the Church of England was not, perhaps also as a legacy of the eighteenth century. Synods were to be the gift of Ireland to world Anglicanism, though in the nineteenth century Ireland did gain something from the examples of the synods of the church overseas. And the relationship between clergy and laity was closer in Church of Ireland tradition; this also may have been a survival of the eighteenth century.

Presbyterians in Ireland were not as in Scotland, for which both parties have been thankful. In fact Irish Presbyterianism has an uncanny appearance of Scottish Presbyterianism through the looking-glass. New Lights in Scotland were Old Lights in Ireland and vice versa, and if the main event in modern Scottish religious history was the Evangelicals being driven out of the church, in Ireland the Evangelicals were able to drive the others out. The Synod of Ulster had begun in 1642, being derived from Scottish settlers to an extent that the Church of Ireland had never been dependent on English settlers. In the eighteenth century there was the usual growth of Deism, and of Moderatism, which eventually drove most Presbyterians in the other direction and made it very difficult for the remnant who would not subscribe to the Westminster Confession. From 1721 onwards these formed the Presbytery of Antrim, vaguely related to the Synod, and in 1829 they joined with Non-Subscribers ejected from or encouraged to leave the Synod of Ulster to form a Remonstrant Synod. This then justified the suspicions of its enemies by becoming Unitarian in its later and declining days. Meanwhile Seceder Presbyterians had multiplied in Ulster, drawing on the Scottish Seceder movement though lacking the Scottish indignation over patronage which had never existed in Ireland. In fact the Irish, and the Canadian and American, success of the Seceder movement is often taken as evidence that the Seceders were born of theological roots rather than of resistance to patronage. In 1840 these Seceders united with the now purified Synod of Ulster to form a church proud of its rigidity and fearful of heresy, though it must be admitted that the continued Deist influence in Ireland made the edginess of Irish Presbyterians less paranoid than outsiders have sometimes supposed.

But Irish Presbyterians have always nurtured a sense of tragedy. They believed they were entitled to the same status in Ireland that they had enjoyed in Scotland, and that they had been betrayed. Of course they *had* been betrayed, but they thought there was something which someone could do about it. Furthermore, they believed they were the real Christians, and indeed the real Irish, since the Church of Ireland was only a system of jobbery, and Roman Catholicism not a religion at all, and they could not understand why people did not see things as they did. In 1834 they were only a tenth the size of the Roman Catholic church in Ireland, and only three-quarters the size of the Church of Ireland, but then it was not numbers that mattered. As contractual relationships ceased to lie at the basis of political life, and numbers began to matter more, their status changed, but to this they were never reconciled.

It has been said that the idea of the Irish nation was first held by the Church of Ireland, then by the Presbyterians, and finally by the Roman Catholics who still keep custody of it. But Roman Catholicism in Ireland as elsewhere has had to change with the times, even if the part of the population which was to be Roman Catholic had been determined from the seventeenth century onwards. It has been argued that it was only in the nineteenth century that the great mass of the Irish people became practising Catholics, but it might equally be argued that a large proportion of any nationality only became practising Christians of any sort in that century. It could also be argued that Irish Catholicism of an earlier age was good enough for its time, but could not be recognized after the theological revolution of the 1840s. It was the critical Synod of Thurles in 1850 which established modern Catholicism, with the rules which made the clergy a class apart, instead of members of families who had an interest in the church. Again, saying mass in barns or private houses was forbidden; the church was expressed in the building of churches. New devotions were introduced, and sacramental life emphasized. With a more modern approach came English in the place of Gaelic, initially in response to popular demand, though it is not clear how this was related to religion.

Much of this advance was associated with Rome, and much of it with Cardinal Cullen. Irish but long resident in Rome, he was sent to bring his homeland into line with the new Ultramontanism (a word for looking 'over the mountains' to Rome for everything). Cullen was violently opposed to the old tolerance of Catholics and Protestants, to the threat of Protestant evangelism which was in fact never very real, and to religion mixed with nationalism, which he associated with the old interference of governments in church affairs. He was also somewhat unrealistic; he believed in 1868 that if the Church of Ireland was disestablished by government it would disappear, and 'all Ireland would soon become Catholic'. It was taken for granted by Cullen and by many more that Irish Protestantism was artificial: a mixture of politics and Freemasonry, imposed on Ireland by outside forces and incapable of any action or devotion of its own. Yet Cullen remade the Irish Catholic church by appointments of bishops in his own mould, and he and his like produced a new Catholic culture. To some he was seen as a tyrant, but the truth is that Irish Catholics did clip his wings when he went too far, and he would never have been able to do anything at all had not the bulk of Irish Catholics been anxious for the new ways which he and others brought to them.

So much for Rome in Ireland, but Rome in Rome had wider visions and wilder worries. Rome was supposed by the British government to have greater political influence in Ireland than was actually the case, and this influence it could use in exchange for British support against Italian nationalists seeking to take over the Papal States. In fact, Cullen was not the only one to see Irish and Italian nationalism in similar terms, but if there was an implied compact it really did no one much good. On the other hand, it did little harm either, and it was inspired by the highest motives. Spiritual independence was a basic tenet of the nineteenth century, and not just amongst Catholics. And if Rome was saved, it was presumed that Rome would be saved for the good of Irish Catholics as well as others.

Yet Irish church life had a momentum of its own, as had Irish nationalism, and in a strange sort of way each supported the other like opposing teams pulling a rope in a tug-of-war. Thus if the bishops and clergy called on their people to do something considered to be in the political sphere, they went unheeded, for in Catholic Ireland there was a separation of religion and politics which was the ideal of the century only rarely achieved elsewhere. And Irish Catholics have never been happy about the idea of theirs being an established religion in Ireland; they have dissociated themselves from any suggestion that Rome should act in concert with London or, later, with Dublin. One of the astonishing things about the Irish bishops since 1922 has been their lack of contact with what is now the Republic of Ireland. In some ways they were drawn into closer relations with the government of Northern Ireland, which had British ideals of church-state relations.

Perhaps Northern Ireland should have the last word in this chapter. If history has a part in that conflict, there is more than history to be considered. When Harold Wilson was prime minister of Britain he urged the Irish to forget their ancient quarrels and, by implication, to be like the English. It is a common approach to Ireland, and by assuming that discord comes from some dark racial memory of ancient wrongs it distracts the mind from wrongs which are far from ancient. It is true that there are differences between the Irish which are religious, and differences which are philosophical, and differences which depend on which century is seen to be the golden age of Ireland's past. But there are also differences which are part of the present social structure, and if these appeal to history for their justification this does not make them historical. That so much of Ireland's troubles are blamed on history implies that the Irish are not so much governed by sensible decisions as by deep grievances rooted in the sub-conscious, and ultimately this means that the Irish cannot be expected to behave as others do. Until this attitude is overcome the real grievances cannot be overcome. When the grievances are overcome then Ireland's history may run in other ways.

9

America, Canada, Australia, New Zealand

In the making of the United States, of Canada, of Australia and of New Zealand, British ideals and customs replaced those of other immigrant groups. (The only real exceptions to this process have been Afrikaners in South Africa, which really lies outside this chapter, and the French in Canada, and both those groups were present in force before the British arrived.) But the one British institution which did not prevail was British religion, if there was such a thing. In fact there never has been a British church, though attempts have been made to create such a thing, notably in the seventeenth century, and we should therefore speak of English or Irish or Scottish religion. That there was no British religion is not, however, the reason that other ethnic groups did not change their religion; there is no British law and there is no British banking system and there is no British educational system, but most colonies took English law and Scottish banking and English or Scottish schooling.

If America is a good place to begin, it can be said that the picture of religious life in America is one of stability. It begins in New England, with a near monopoly by the Congregationalists which obscured an underlying diversity. Out of New England Congregationalism came Presbyterian and Episcopal churches in proportions more recognizable in Britain than in New England, and in due course Methodists were to be added. If the Churches of Christ or Disciples of Christ seem to be a new tradition, they can be seen as Scottish Seceders expressing the sacramental teachings of the 1840s. Only Pentecostalism does not fit the pattern found elsewhere, but Pentecostalism is neither uniform nor all that large. There are innumerable small denominations in America, but they have remained small. And if religion is stable in America, it is also stable in Canada, Australia and New Zealand.

If the first characteristic to be noted is stability, there is also a tendency to be intellectually barren. The mother churches in the British Isles have been surpassed by daughter churches in vitality and organization and outreach and social concern, but of original theology they have been content to have little. It is common to say that America only produced one original theologian, Jonathan Edwards. It is not common to suggest that one cause of his brilliance may have been his rejection of the old world as a religious force, 'as that continent has crucified Christ, they shall not have the honour of communicating religion in its most glorious state to us, but we to them . . .' Indeed, he took the words of Isaiah 60.19, 'Surely the isles shall wait for me . . .', and wrote, 'I cannot think that anything else can be here intended but America.' Perhaps more of such bad scholarship would have inspired Americans to produce good scholarship.

If there is no British religion, there is Anglican religion. It was never strong overseas. Emigration from Britain in the early days tended to be Scottish or Irish rather than English, and when the English finally arrived they found a social or religious structure already closed to them. And by the time that the English arrived, they had absorbed the doctrines of a new upper class trained in public schools and considered to be acceptable to all, since the new upper class included the Scottish and Irish upper classes, though assimilation failed lower down the social scale. Of colonial bishops it was said in 1865, 'The colonists of all denominations are sensible of the advantages which they enjoy in being able to obtain the services in positions of influence of men who have received a first-class English education . . .' Of course many were not sensible of these advantages, but others were, and Anglicans found this to be a means of entry into colonial societies, though that means of entry later proved an embarrassment. And the emphasis on bishops came to be regarded as just a religious cloak for upper-class claims. Sometimes it was, but sometimes it was not.

As English religious dominance took hold in the colonies, Presbyterianism in Canada and Roman Catholicism in Australia came to be identified with democracy as Anglicanism was not. Yet in the Canadas the democratic opposition to a rather weak Anglican establishment was Methodist and itself English. But the social functions of Methodism are as arguable in Canada as they are in England. On the face of it, a populist Methodism from the United States swept into the Canadas and challenged Anglicanism. Yet that same Methodism was forced, if it wanted popular support, to affiliate with the most hierarchical and conservative

brand of British Methodism, the Wesleyan. It did not so much challenge
the Church of England as seek to replace it by conforming to its ways.
And here we find a characteristic of Methodism in the new world. It was
fluid. It could flow into new territory, but it always adapted to the
terrain.

But that leads to a wider tendency of English religion, whether Anglican or Methodist. It usually travelled best in Scottish or Irish bottles.
When Canadian Methodists and the few Congregationalists united with
most of the Presbyterians in 1925, the result was supposed to be something quite new, but in fact turned out to be more Presbyterian than
anything else. Admittedly the union was followed by a world-wide swing
to theological conservativism which favoured Presbyterians rather than
Methodists, but there does seem to have been a general willingness to
let the English heritage go under and to conserve the Scottish. And
Anglican experience in Canada has also pointed to something similar.
Probably most Anglicans in Canada are English or partly English in
origin, but many eastern dioceses are partly, and four are overwhelmingly, Church of Ireland in background. It has been said of some
mythical bishop in the Canadas during the 1860s that on one day he
would find a group of English settlers humbly requesting that he provide
them with a vicar, a church, a school and a vicarage. Next day he would
find a group of Irish settlers violently demanding that he find them a
rector to occupy the rectory they had built and to minister in the church
they were building. And, to complete, the story, that bishop would have
been a Scot, as so many were.

When J. K. Galbraith was American ambassador in India he remarked that the British Commonwealth was only taken seriously as a
practical force in the two and a half cities of London, Washington and
Canberra. The same might be said of the Anglican Communion, if we
substitute the one and two quarters cities of London, Canterbury and
York. This does not mean that any Anglicans are against the Anglican
Communion; since most of them do not expect it to do anything they
cannot oppose it. It only has to be there, and that is enough. And if the
English think of it as in some sense an extension of themselves, that
troubles nobody. There have been occasional collisions between various
views, as in 1893 when the Canadians took the title 'archbishop' and
notified the Archbishop of Canterbury on what he described as a half-
sheet of foreign notepaper. It took him two years to accept what had
been done. But the Anglican Communion is largely symbolic, and has
resisted all attempts to turn it into something practical.

The importance of Irish Roman Catholicism cannot be exaggerated, despite many attempts to do this. And in this matter the timing was critical. Had famine struck a generation earlier the world might have been filled with Irish sceptics, rather than Irish Catholic zealots. Even as it was, it is clear that many Irish migrants were not converted to the new Catholicism of the 1840s until after they had settled overseas. Furthermore, it was vital that the Irish should migrate when they did. Had the first wave of Catholic arrivals in America been Lithuanians and Poles and Germans and Italians, they would have found a nation already formed without them, and it would have taken them all that much longer to find their place in American life as they learned English. Roman Catholicism in America would have been regarded as was Eastern Orthodoxy; an exotic survival of ancient societies now in decline.

Of all places where the Irish went, Australia is the most fascinating. That only Roman Catholics in Australia have written church history must mean something, though it must also mean something that they have only written church history. But that history is heady stuff, and the facts are sufficiently startling even before we come to the theories. We find English Benedictines trying to create a model church in which all clergy will be monks, secure in the conviction that, as Englishmen, they were 'superior to all party spirit . . .' This dream collapses as the English fail to supply priests, while the Irish supply them in plenty. Next comes the attempt to build a new Ireland in the Southern Hemisphere, with Cardinal Cullen of Dublin putting his nephews and family friends into Australian bishoprics five at a time. We find bishops at war with each other, with their priests, with Rome, with governments, and with just about anyone and anything. In the history as written by Cardinal Moran it was all magnificent and successful, but a later historian calls it 'mindless pragmatism'. It was probably not mindless; it was certainly not pragmatic. It was a dream from an age of dreamers, and it faded with the light of day, leaving Australian Catholics wondering where they went wrong. But this is something in which not only Catholics are involved, for over Australian religious history there hangs a brooding sense of failure. C. M. H. Clark writes of believers in the kingdom of heaven who became members of the kingdom of nothingness, but whatever Australia is about, it is more than that. And the Irish fact is comparable to the Irish fact elsewhere; the interweaving of romantic Catholicism with democratic rationalism, seen in the revolt at Eureka Hill in 1854, could only last so long, and if it has now started to unravel, then Australia will doubtless weave something else in its place.

Moving from the Irish to the Scots, there is a common pattern to the denominations of Presbyterianism in all lands. Furthermore, this is common to Methodism as well, and it has been argued that nineteenth-century Presbyterianism was not particularly Scottish in its expressions of a world-wide Evangelicalism. Certainly the denominational divisions do not begin in Scotland and spread out as loyal Scots overseas support whatever is happening at home. It went far deeper than that. To take the example of the Seceders: if the Scottish Seceders first seceded over patronage, Seceder churches flourished most in countries which had never known patronage, and this supports the view that locally Scottish issues were not at the root of this movement. On the other hand, the famous Disruption of 1843 in which the Free Church was born was not just a response to muddle-headedness in the Scottish legal system, but was part of a world-wide assertion of a new theological imperative. Presbyterianianism, even more than most religious systems, has shown an ability to replicate itself in all its manifold variations in any country to which a single cell has been taken by migration. If early Canadian Presbyterianism was largely Seceder, this did not prevent the Established, the Free, the Seceder and the American brands all taking root as the country developed, and not just by migration from Scotland. Similarly, though later in history, the New Zealand Presbyterians were virtually all linked to the Free Church of Scotland in the early days of the colony, but this did not prevent later divisions between the Northern Church on the one hand and the Synod of Otago and Southland on the other, parallel to the Seceder and Free traditions in Scotland, or to New School and Old School in America. As if in some biological experiment, the churches of all lands divided and then rejoined without an external model to copy.

If there is a sameness about churchly matters, there is a more limited sameness about attitudes to society. It is limited by the belief that America is a special place, and that it is there that God's kingdom will be most clearly seen. This may have had roots in the moralistic Calvinism of Jonathan Edwards and the New England revival, or in a moralistic constitution from a moralistic age, or in the unrestricted influence of a Protestant clergy in what was almost entirely a Protestant country. But the devotion of American Christians to social objectives owed much to the fact that they had in slavery a divisive social institution which could not be ignored. American Protestantism was shaped by the battle against slavery, but American Catholicism was not, since it had little influence in those days. If the abolition of slavery was presented as a religious crusade, and is still so presented in the 'Battle Hymn of the Republic', the Protestant churches found themselves still geared to social reform when that battle was over. They moved to the problems of the inner cities, which by this time were largely inhabited by non-Protestants whom Protestants could scarcely influence, and to the problem of alcohol. If America stumbled over the Prohibition of alcoholic drink, this was in part because it was wrongly identified with the problem of slavery, though it could be argued that the Emancipation Proclamation was only the first step towards solving that problem and the last is not yet in sight. But this heritage has divided Protestants from Catholics; Catholics in America have been more concerned with their own survival in an unfriendly environment, and now that the environment is no longer unfriendly they are unaccustomed to looking critically upon it. They have not had the experience of the fight against slavery. But in recent years they have more than made up for this failure, and their bishops are so outspoken on social concerns that they might as well be Protestants.

In studying the whole phenomenon of immigrant churches, the clergy are obviously of prime importance. In all denominations the need for colonial clergy was met by lowering standards. Irish overseas priests were trained at All Hallows, and these were often the men who would not have been accepted at Maynooth for work in Ireland itself; their uncouth manners were to offend the laity even in roughest Australia. Presbyterians were recruited in Scotland and Ireland, though a few of the Scots sent to Canada turned out to seek nothing but a free passage, and two proved to be imposters and not ministers at all. As for the Anglicans, the Colonial Clergy Act of 1874 allowed Englishmen to be ordained in churches overseas provided they stayed there and did not try to creep back into the Church of England. This Act has sometimes been attacked as an insult to overseas clergy, but in fact it gave overseas churches clergy who could not be tempted away, and it effectively destroyed the idea of a single Church of England extending throughout the world.

Clergy of this sort were cheap and plentiful and most of them did good work, and in the days of actual immigration it was natural that such men should be imported along with everyone else. But in later days they remained cheap and they remained plentiful; this made it unnecessary for local candidates to be properly trained, and when such local candidates were trained it was to the lower level of the half-educated imports. Yet as the overseas nations developed, they created educational systems which surpassed those in Britain. However, if they excelled in other disciplines they did not do so in theology. There is a factor here which cannot be pinned down. Despite heroic efforts to advance the study of religion in America and other countries deriving that religion from Britain, those efforts have come to little. The ecclesiastical landscape is littered with Manhattan projects which never reached critical mass. Except, of course, for Jonathan Edwards in his lonely study on the Massachusetts frontier, which returns us to our beginnings.

10

Church and Society

If something is wrong, and something always is, then it is natural to try and find a cause. And it is tempting to try and find a simple case which can be simply corrected. We can thus convince ourselves that it is unusual for anything to go wrong, that this is really quite a happy and a simple sort of world, and we can sit back and enjoy it.

So it is with church and society. If people do not come to church, then there must be a reason, and it is simpler to refer to one reason than to a whole set of reasons. And if we want a reason which will not worry us too much, it is best to blame things on the dead. Church leaders of the past did not speak out against social abuses, and people stopped going to church. It is as simple as that, and we can stop worrying. All that we have to do is to denounce dead church leaders and make positive noises about social reform, and the situation will right itself. People will come back to church.

Obviously, there are a lot of assumptions in this. It is assumed that people will be naturally interested in Christianity if there is no unnatural obstacle to that interest. It is assumed that full churches are normal. It is also assumed that people as a whole are not very bright. If they were bright in times past, then they could have distinguished between the Christian faith on the one hand and the social policies of certain church leaders on the other. Moreover, if they were bright today then they could distinguish between the social campaigns of the churches and Christianity, and take the social campaigns without the Christianity. In fact this whole point of view also assumes that the population as a whole cannot appreciate the Christian faith but can understand long queues for surgical treatment and must therefore be brought to Christianity through what they really do understand. It may also be argued that it is not frank, apart from being not very sensible, to campaign for social reform when the ultimate aim is to fill churches. However, it must be admitted that the people who undertake such campaigns are usually not clear enough in their thinking to be deliberately deceitful, and they really want social reform anyway.

Yet the assumption which most concerns us is that at some time in recent history there was a clear opportunity for Christians to do something decisive in the social field, and this opportunity was not taken. Instead, Christians either did nothing or supported the rich against the poor. This is a highly debatable view of history, and yet it is seldom debated. If it proves to be untrue, then a whole set of notions on which much present church work is based will crumble to dust.

An obvious example concerns the Highland Clearances in Scotland. The prevailing view is that the Highland people lived a happy and democratic life until the lairds went down to London, lived above their means, and to pay their debts drove out the people and imported sheep for more profit. This view is attractive in blaming things on London, but it does not explain why the Highlanders went quietly, so the ministers of the Kirk are brought into the story. They were nominated by the lairds and so they told the people that if they resisted the Clearances they would end up in Hell, and that was that. Now we know why people in Scotland are falling away from the church.

Yet Scottish historians always were a bit sceptical about this, and recently scholars have presented a quite different account. It is an account of population rising beyond the resources of the land, of failed attempts to diversify the Highland economy, of landowners having to reduce the population or lose their estates to speculators, and of Highland tenants voluntarily emigrating in large numbers even before landlords realized that emigration was desirable. Of course the move from the land occurred all over Europe; if it was sometimes harder for Highlanders than others, it was because their remoteness made it more of a shock for them than for other rural groups. And if there were heartless landlords and heartless evictions, there were also craven ministers, but the evidence presented by historians with no interest in religion is much more favourable to the ministers than the evidence presented by modern churchmen seeking a scapegoat. Nonetheless, as long as there is a need for a simple explanation of modern secularism, the story of the minister serving to move the tenants for the benefit of the landowner will survive and flourish.

But here we must move on to a specific historian, E. R. Norman, who seems to enjoy infuriating Christians of the left but still has something

to say. In his book, *Church and Society in England 1770–1970,* he insists
that the social ideas of churchmen were 'derived from the surrounding
intellectual and political culture and not, as churchmen themselves
always tend to assume, from theological learning'. Up to a point he is
probably right about this, but there is a fatal flaw to his argument, as
will be seen later. Specifically, Norman asserts that for much of the early
nineteenth century Christians were hampered by belief in the 'unseen
hand' of political economy. If the economic system was a basic part of
the creation, it would cause untold misery to interfere with its workings,
and any misery which already existed must be due to existing interference. Later in the nineteenth century Christian leaders had moved to
a view of society in which they could interfere for the public good, but
by then most of the population had caught up with the Adam Smith
views of the 'unseen hand' which the leaders had now dropped. Thus
the academics and church leaders were always out of step with the
masses whom they wished to assist, though Norman is not clear on
whether this mattered in the long run or not. However, it is hard to
reject his conclusion that, 'Each generation of Christians offers up in
each age what they judge most to convey the presence of Christ. A lot
of what is transient gets caught up in the process.'

Yet even in Norman there is an underlying assumption that the
nineteenth-century church must have done something wrong. It may be
because the clergy and the people had different social ideas, or had the
same ones at different times. It may be because so many of the clergy
were themselves of the upper classes, though there is no evidence that
those clergy who were not of the upper classes did any better. And yet
the attempt to identify the trouble is a sign that the trouble is not really
taken seriously. The trouble is the trouble. History is trouble, and life
is troublesome.

If the writing of E. R. Norman must be used to clear our minds of
what computer experts call clutter, this still does not tell us what the
churches did. But, if we are to give a short answer, they did what
Norman says they did. They followed the political or economic wis-
dom of the day, which is hardly surprising. The New Testament can
hardly be described as providing a developed political theory. It may
call on Christians to show concern for their neighbours, but it does
not write this concern into specific legislation. The result is that Christians become involved in social movements instead of having their own
social movements. Even the Evangelicals of Clapham in the early nineteenth century collaborated with Unitarians and the well-meaning

irreligious to attain their social goals, and this has been the same ever since.

Yet there is a sense in which the entire E. R. Norman argument falls flat on its face. Norman is assuming that Christian ideology and secular ideology are separate, and in this he is himself a product of an era when the 'two kingdoms' thought-patterns of the Gothic Revival and its successors were widespread. It would be wrong to assume that Christians went to the New Testament to discover the best system of health insurance; they went to the London School of Economics. But the New Testament sent them to the social scientists in the first place, and countless generations of Christian thought had so influenced everything in the country that basic beliefs on civic duties and on the dignity of the individual person lay behind whatever could be found at the London School of Economics. Nor does the Norman analysis fall flat on this issue alone: the New Testament does provide a means of discriminating between rival economic or political theories, and there are rival social theories and always have been. One theory may be dominant in a particular era, but it is never exclusive, and even the dominant theory will usually appear in different forms. The interaction of religious and secular thought is a far more complex process than is usually imagined.

Of course there have been times when churches agitated in their own interests. Non-conformists understandably battled through most of the nineteenth century for the removal of such restrictions as still weighed upon them, and in their way so did Roman Catholics. The established churches of England and Scotland had less need to lobby Parliament, but they did so when their interests were at stake. On the whole they showed more concern for society, not because they were more virtuous, but because they were more involved in the wider establishment. They had, or were thought to have, more responsibility for what happened. This may be seen in the complaint that Roman Catholic gentry were not concerned about the evils of industrial society. Their response would have been that they were not responsible for industrial society; when England was Catholic it was not industrial.

Moving on to this century, one of the figures most quoted on church and society is William Temple, who was Archbishop of Canterbury at the time of his death in 1944. Temple spent much of his life on the problems of society, and his paperback *Christianity and the Social Order*, published in 1942, was extremely popular in its day. It is much criticized, when it is even remembered, in ours. Yet Temple's paperback was never intended to be taken that seriously. It was produced very rapidly and it was published just when millions of Britons wondered if the end of the war would lead to more of the same sort of life they had had before, or whether things might get better. Temple said they could be better, and in this he was right. And Temple was not as mindlessly hopeful as is sometimes suggested. About south-east Europe he did write, 'If, on the other hand, all could be brought to love their neighbours as themselves, there would be no problem', but he did not suggest that this was going to come easily, if it would come at all.

Against Temple, it must be said that his notion of past history led him astray. He thought that in the ages just before his own there had been a withdrawal of the church from public life, and there had been a concentration on the individual to the exclusion of society, which he blamed on Calvinism. These features he saw as unusual, and a church which had a social policy he considered to be normal. But if his readers could accept that the church should have a social policy, the policy recommended by Temple was much more realistic than some critics have suggested. His central point was the dignity of the human person, and that the human person is social flowed from the relationship with God. But having said that, Temple distanced himself from particular patterns of government. He was concerned with the moral consequences of social and economic policies, not their effectiveness for their own purposes, since he held that the welfare of people was the aim of such policies. And with a healthy distrust of large associations, he defended the 'lesser associations', which, as he put it, 'do not quite fit any theoretical pattern', but which, particularly in education, are useful in 'checking the tendency of a mass-age to bureaucracy'. Temple showed himself in this brief work to be realistic about human nature, and realistic about society, but he was still hopeful. It was perhaps the very limits to his hopes which made him acceptable to a wide public in his day.

If we are now to look at history as it is usually presented, we find a number of people who are regarded as early Christian socialists. Usually they were nothing of the kind. They were late paternalists. They had not looked forward beyond the theories of Adam Smith and the 'unseen hand'; they had been brought up in such backward circumstances as not even to have heard of Adam Smith. If Shaftesbury could argue for government intervention in the market place, it was because he was so thoroughly out of date that he did not even know there was a market place. If F. D. Maurice could advocate some sort of Christian commonwealth, it was because he really belonged to the Middle Ages. Yet there was a point at which the old paternalists did give way to the new socialists. And the vision of a new society, solidly anchored in Christian doctrine, was very largely replaced by a vision of humanity which owed little to classical Christianity. If it was not based on the full-blown theory of the goodness of man, as extolled by Dickens, then it depended upon the liberal Protestantism of the nineteenth century.

This may be seen in the figure of Keir Hardie, an early socialist sometimes cited as an example of Christianity in action. Yet Hardie has been more convincingly described as a man who believed in fellowship and justice and in the goodness and decency of most people. People would be happy if they were not oppressed, and the oppression really did not help anybody. If this was the case, there was nobody who would fight for the system once it was seen for what it was, and there was thus no need for violence or revolution, and it was this view as much as anything else which accounted for the peaceful and progressive nature of British socialism. There is a song associated with the early socialist propagandists of the journal *Clarion*, who roamed the countryside on bicycles, 'Nailing down lies and disposing of fables, Improving the landscape by sticking up labels.' And many church people, as well as many unchurched socialists, believed that it was just a matter of labels. This was only to be expected in a society in which the sense of human goodness was widespread while the sense of sin was weak. Conflict could never be due to a difference of interests; better understanding could lead to a better world for everyone, and better understanding was achieved by sticking up labels. There was no sense of progress being bought at a price, or that the improvement of the lot of the poor would only be achieved by some sacrifice, voluntary or otherwise, on the part of the rich. Similarly, it was not recognized that conflict in international affairs concerned real differences in which one party or another had to suffer some sort of loss. In the language of the day, conflict was an artificial concept. There was no such thing.

Yet the prevailing optimism was not entirely unjustified. There were in Britain, as elsewhere, a sufficient number of the well-off who believed that it was better to live at a somewhat reduced standard of living in a society which was not torn against itself and in which they were not forced to tolerate the suffering which injustice produced around them. There was a belief that a better society would benefit everyone. And reforms were undertaken, and the quality of life did improve, even if it did not improve enough. But at the end of the day there were still such appalling injustices and areas of urban poverty and hopelessness that an easy optimism became impossible. That there was something seriously wrong with the human race was to become, once again, a serious proposition. And one for which a theology was needed.

- II -

Darwin and Creation

Whether by accident or design, the universe is there. But whether it is there by accident or design has always mattered. If our forefathers inherited from the eighteenth century a universe from which you could determine what sort of God had created it, then it mattered if you found that whoever or whatever made the world did so by chance. And if you had inherited a system in which God was mainly a creator, then you would have a high view of the creation and you would consider it to be permanent just because it reflected an unchanging God. The world had to be solid if God was solid. But if you had a constantly changing world, instead of a very solid one, then this suggested a constantly changing God. And if the world was made by accident, then it was suggested that God did not care enough about people to make them, but just took them on when they happened to appear. Charles Hodge wrote in 1874 that 'the denial of design in nature is virtually the denial of God', and if he was untypical amongst theologians, even conservative theologians, in saying this, it does tell us something of the limited ideas of God which could then exist.

In fact it was time for a change. The old eighteenth-century view of everything being solid had to give way to the new nineteenth-century view of everything growing and changing. This happened in literature and art and theology, and it happened in science. On the whole people made the adjustment without too much trouble, but if somebody was left with an eighteenth-century view of religion and a nineteenth-century view of science, then their gears would not mesh. And of course it would be just as bad to have a nineteenth-century view of religion and an eighteenth-century view of science, though in either case it could be possible for most people to keep their religion and their science in separate compartments.

The old way in biology may be seen in Linnaeus, the eighteenth-century Swedish classifier of plants. His system was so perfect that in a real garden he even arranged all sorts of plants in classifications according to his theories, which nature had unfortunately neglected to do. It was static. The same species had existed since the beginning and always would.

There is a half-way position seen in Lamarck, a Frenchman who did believe in change, but failed to see how it worked. His 'first law' was that organs such as eyes or limbs developed if you used them, so that if you live in a dark cave your eyes wither away, and if you run away from tigers your legs grow stronger. His second law was that whatever you develop may be inherited by your descendants, if you can run fast enough to survive and have any. Thus the first giraffes stretched their necks to reach high branches of trees, and later giraffes were born with pre-stretched necks, though the process did not seem to work backwards by giraffes in zoos having baby giraffes with pre-shrunk necks suitable for eating out of buckets. In fact the process does not work at all; Lamarck is only worth mentioning so that we can see that this is not Darwin's theory at all.

And so to Charles Darwin. The key thing to understand about him is that he was or had been religious in the eighteenth-century sense, but scientific in the nineteenth-century sense. This may have occurred because he was going round the world with the *Beagle* during the key years when that same world switched from a static eighteenth-century to a changing nineteenth-century outlook. Furthermore, there is a tendency for those who have left their homeland to fix in their memories that homeland as they have left it, and thus to be unable to adjust to changes which have occurred in their absence. From 1831 until 1836 Darwin was abroad, and his scientific world was changing, but not his religious world. That his scientific world changed due to his observations is only partly true: he had read Lyell's geology, in which a long time-scale was necessary for evolution; and he had read Malthus, who argued that population grew faster than did food supplies, which implied that the creation was not benevolent, as people were intended to starve or kill off the surplus. As Darwin remarked of Malthus' view of nature, 'It is difficult to believe in the dreadful but quiet war of organic beings going on in the peaceful woods and smiling fields.' But believe it he did, and rather than attribute it to God he may have preferred to attribute it to chance.

After his return to England in 1836, Darwin waited twenty years before writing *The Origin of Species*. It is not clear why. He continued his research while enjoying a happy family life withdrawn from fashionable society. He became something of an invalid, perhaps from some bug in a Chilean river, or perhaps from bouts of depression. His religion faded gradually, and he decided that he was agnostic, though he avoided discussion on this subject. Depression may have had something to do with this, or it may have been the difficulty of relating religion from one era, to science from another, as suggested above, or it may have been for some quite different reason. But it is not clear whether his retreat from religion was related to his scientific discoveries.

Although he had worked out early drafts of *The Origin of Species*, Darwin was only pushed into publishing in 1859 by a scholar in Malaya who had reached similar conclusions. His book was an instant success, though it shocked some, as he blurred the distinctions between different species. There is an echo of this in the Alice-in-Wonderland incident where Alice finds gardeners in a bed of white roses 'busily painting them red'. Furthermore, Darwin did not believe in the balance of nature which so many regarded as basic, and to which some modern ecological enthusiasts would wish to return, but rather in a nature which changed through natural selection. This meant that under population pressure the more suitable types survived, while the others did not. There is an echo of this also in Alice, with the bread-and-butter fly, which lives on weak tea with cream in it, and, without that diet, 'it would die of course'. Alice comments, 'But that must happen very often,' and is answered, 'It always happens.' Such was a dead end in evolution. But there were gaps in Darwin's argument, though some of the gaps were filled by the rediscovery of Mendel's genetics, which showed how variations occurred. However, natural selection is the sort of theory which we should not expect to be proved. It can be shown to be probable, but that is all.

Reaction was mainly amongst scientists, as might have been expected, and in those days many scientists were clergymen. Much has been made of a meeting of the British Association in 1860 at which Bishop Wilberforce was rebuked by T. H. Huxley for asking if he claimed to be descended from an ape through his grandfather or grandmother. This discussion may well have happened, though no formal record exists, and nobody seems to have thought much about it. Of course Darwin never suggested that human beings were descended from apes; he suggested that both were descended from a common ancestor. Nonetheless, the evidence would suggest that most churchmen accepted Darwin's theory fairly painlessly. Even that Charles Hodge who rejected it in 1874 had an equally devout and learned son who implicitly accepted it. And when the founding fathers of Fundamentalism published the pamphlets called *The Fundamentals* early in this century, three of the essays accepted evolution, though two did not.

It has been argued that many of those Christians who rejected Darwinism did so not because it threatened their religion but because it threatened their science. However, it was unlikely that many ordinary Christians then, any more than ordinary Christians now, really had much idea of science. It has also been argued that some who took up Darwin's ideas were still so soaked in the idea of the Great Architect as creator of all things according to a single system that they believed that if God had used natural selection to produce organic variations, then he must have used it for everything. Thus survival of the fittest could be held to dominate economics, war, and football. This was to use the theory as Darwin himself did not; he thought natural selection was the main way in which variation had occurred in human history, but he did not think that it was the only way. He specifically rejected the idea that it was the main way once civilization had begun and communities could exercise some control over their futures.

But Darwin had not finished. In 1871 he published another book called *The Descent of Man*. If his first book suggested that group interests moved the individual, his second book was stronger on individual choices (usually that of a mate) influencing the group. In fact it was all about choice, and the 1870s were a time in which people were obsessed about choice. However, this book supposed that there must be a surplus of women in every society, since without any surplus almost everyone would be chosen anyway. Furthermore, it ignored hidden genes, which are so well hidden that nobody really knows whose offspring will be best. But *The Descent of Man* attracted little attention from the world of religion. Had it done so it might even have received approval for conferring dignity on man as having free choice.

The negative religious reaction to Darwin, such as it was, may be summed up under three headings. Some decided that the thing was not new; it was the old enemy Deism in a modern form. The trouble with 'the best of all possible worlds' view of our world is that our world does not seem, to people actually living in it, to be all that good. Darwin's theory meant that it could now be argued that if it is not the best of all possible worlds it soon will be, thanks to evolution. The old self-regulating universe had become self-improving as well, and was bound to get better and better, and so would men and women. There would be no need for a saviour and no need for salvation, as the tides of time carried everyone on to perfection, moral as well as other.

The second negative reaction came from recognizing that Darwin's world was immoral, as he had noted with dismay on reading Malthus. The same dismay is found in Alice, in a new version of the eighteenth-century bit of doggerel that ran, 'How doth the busy little bee, Improve each shining hour, And gather honey all the day, From every opening flower.' That was a nice happy world in which people copied nature by working away in the sunshine, but the Alice version sketched in a world which was not only frightening but pretended to be other than it was. 'How doth the little crocodile, Improve his shining tail, And pour the waters of the Nile, On every golden scale! How cheerfully he seems to grin, Now neatly spreads his claws, And welcomes little fishes in, With gently smiling jaws.'

The third negative reaction was also moral, and this concerned the loss of personal identity. If we are for ever changing, do we have an identity? If we are not the same persons that we were yesterday, are we responsible for what we did then? As Alice said to the caterpillar, 'I know who I *was* when I got up this morning, but I must have changed several times since then.'

Yet there were gains for Christian thought as well as losses. If natural selection said that the world as we have it is dreadful, Christians had argued this against the older Deists who said that it was wonderful. And natural selection did enable man to see himself as a partner with nature. Moreover, in the course of time it came to be realized that natural selection of the Darwinian type was not all that important in our world anyway. It works too slowly. Darwin himself had said this, and the whole of what we call history has happened far too rapidly for the slow processes of natural selection to have had any effect. Natural selection is about our past, not our present, and not our future. As for the present and the future, Lamarck's discredited theory, about the giraffe stretching his neck, has been proved true in a way which he could not have foreseen. Knowledge can be passed from one generation to another, and while we may not have developed improved legs or improved eyes, we have developed bicycles and spectacles.

However, the main change is found not in biology but in physics. A constant complaint against teaching evolution in the schools has been that it is not proven fact, but only a theory. But if it was normal to think of science as fact in the past, it is not so now. Since Max Planck and

Einstein and the more radical thinkers of later days there has been a new approach to physics, which has treated the theories as useful guides to reality, rather than actual laws. Furthermore, Max Born has argued for the instability of matter, saying that 'stability and life are incompatible', which is rather like Darwinism in another discipline. This means that we need not complain if it is possible to poke holes in Darwin's theory; it is supposed to have holes in it. If it had no holes it might be less likely to be true. And with a universe which is seen to have holes in it, there is room for God, and room for choice and grace and beauty. Banesh Hoffman wrote about quantum physics in these words: 'When at the empty dawn of creation God created the primal essence energy, he endowed it with such subtle, miraculous potencies that, as a seed that slowly comes to flower, there grew from it what we call space and time and matter and radiation.' And if this sounds something like the eighteenth century all over again, it only sounds that way. The reality is alive and unpredictable, not dead and determined, and in this it is a truer guide to the nature of God.

12

World Mission

'The heathen in his blindness, Bows down to wood and stone.' So wrote Bishop Heber in a hymn which is sometimes thought typical of the Victorian missionary. It is not a good hymn, and it is not good teaching, but it was not even typical of Heber. When he went to India he visited the Hindu holy city of Benares, observed the rituals, and wrote in his journal, 'God may have much people in this city.'

Eighteenth-century beliefs about the non-Christian world can be seen in a series of Scottish sermons given in aid of missionary work. Of non-Christian religions one preacher said they were all 'founded on fear', while another noted that in them, 'Not a trace of truth remains . . .' More typical was a preacher in 1792 who said that 'the primaeval religion of the lapsed world included the great principles of natural religion', of which something remained, while a preacher in 1796 said bluntly, 'The world was never without a divine revelation, and whatsoever was the degree in which it had been given, it seems always to have proceeded from the Son of God.' Of non-Christians another preacher said, 'They are in the hands of a gracious God, who is acquainted with their state . . .', and yet they could be condemned for 'wilful and habitual disobedience to that eternal and universal law which is written in their hearts'. Scots laid more stress than others on the relics of 'natural law', and in mission work they taught natural religion before revealed religion, almost as if they expected Deists to lurk behind palm trees wherever they landed. But in Calcutta the great missionary Alexander Duff did find his work complicated by the teaching of the Indian Deist, Ram Mohan Roy, even if his experience was unusual.

It has been argued that missionaries went to Africa and Asia with cultural baggage; undoubtedly they did. Nobody goes anywhere without cultural baggage, and Christianity can no more live without a culture than bacteria in a laboratory can live without a culture. But the baggage was not always the worst. The history of racism has been mixed with that of missions, and it is hard to see how it could have been otherwise. However, racism as we know it has been a comparatively recent thing. In the late eighteenth century there were a variety of views. There was an Evangelical lobby saying of the black slave, 'Am I not a man and a brother?' There was also a pseudo-scientific group who held that other races were created separately and could not interbreed with Europeans. Mixed with these ideas was the notion that races were created to live in specific climates and would wilt in others; the racist Robert Knox solemnly predicted in a later age that when immigration into America ended, all races would fade away except the original Indians. And if many ideas were fantastic that did not matter; the question was academic, since it was not yet necessary to have a colonial policy. Europeans were only in fleeting contact with other races, and if they wanted to know about them, it was partly to determine the nature of Greek and Roman society, since Africans and Asians were thought to be in the same state as the peoples of classical antiquity.

British racial thinking underwent a transformation in the 1850s when the Indian Mutiny and the Jamaica rebellion meant that Britain had to have some policy, instead of just fanciful thought. What was selected was a compromise. Other races were child races; this meant they were human but they were inferior until they had progressed, which might take a very long time. This view might have had a distant connection with Darwinism, but if it did then it was distant indeed, and the only thing to be said of it was that it served the imperial powers in the short run. If other races had been considered fully equal with Europeans then they could not have been ruled, and if they were not human then they could only have been ruled in ways which led to violent rebellion. The idea of child races avoided both extremes, and the speed of development could be varied, since different races could be regarded as advanced or backward to fit appropriate policies.

Modern missions as we know them really developed in the 1790s when missionary societies were formed in various countries. Until then only small groups, Moravians in Protestantism and Jesuits and Dominicans and Franciscans in Catholicism, engaged in overseas mission. But by the end of the eighteenth century trade with other lands was increasing, and the ideal of the state-church was fading. If every citizen need not be a Christian, every Christian need not be a citizen. And Protestants were especially active if Evangelical, since their faith was more personal and less national.

The London Missionary Society was formed in 1795 as a non-denominational but strictly Evangelical body which promptly bought a ship, recruited twenty missionaries, and shipped them off to the South Seas. It was believed that all they had to do was to convert a small number of people and the thing would soon reach critical mass and that would be that. Furthermore, it was believed that denominational differences would not matter in the mission field and could be ignored.

The awakening was not pleasant. Missionaries divided on doctrinal grounds before they were out of sight of the British coast. Missionaries arrived in the field and died of fever or were murdered. Missionaries discovered the difficulties of missionary work and drifted into trade. Some soldiered on, but it would take many years before they could find or be found by the scattered individuals who wanted to be Christian. And enthusiasm amongst supporters at home became less and less. Many assumed that the missionary cause was already lost.

And then, in the 1820s, it suddenly dawned upon those obstinate losers who were still supporting missions that the enterprise was slowly bearing fruit. Not much fruit, but thirty years of effort had produced handfuls of converts, and some of the converts had produced converts. It was now recognized that mission work would be difficult, but not always impossible. And specific missionary skills came to be identified. In particular, early missionaries needed something to make them useful to those amongst whom they settled if they were to be allowed to settle. Usually that something was medicine, though early European medicine was a doubtful asset. Sometimes it was another skill, such as writing letters for chiefs, or painting wagons, or calculating calendars.

But there was another upheaval in the 1840s when it was discovered that most missions were undertaken by unofficial societies if Protestant, or by religious orders if Catholic. When the doctrine of the church loomed large it was naturally felt that the church should be the missionary body, and it was argued that Christ's promise at the end of St Matthew's Gospel was made to his disciples collectively, and not to a missionary sub-committee. If societies did not entirely disappear, their connection with churches was strengthened, and many churches worked directly in mission. However, in fact this did not make much difference. It did not even bring in much money; right through the golden age of nineteenth-century missions the average congregation only made token contributions. Only a small minority of Christians were ever committed to the missionary enterprise.

If the 1840s stressed the doctrine of the church at home, the 1860s stressed the same doctrine overseas. It was a time when overseas Christians were forming quite large groups, and yet they were not churches but subsidiaries of churches in other lands. The principle of forming new churches in new lands, with self-government and with local customs, was accepted in theory if not always in practice.

But in the last quarter of the nineteenth century much of this last work was undone. A new and violent racism had its effect on missionary thinking as well as on other thinking, though it was fiercely resisted in some quarters. In the 1870s there can be seen a new reliance on European or American leadership. In Bengal the Scottish missionary Alexander Duff had sent his young urban converts out into the villages around Calcutta to create new churches, but when these men were too old to carry on, their replacements in the 1880s were not Indians but Scots. It was said that there were no new Indian leaders to replace the old ones, but by that time Europeans were not given to seeing leadership in Indian character. In Jamaica a young Scottish missionary married a black wife and took her to a mission station in what is now Nigeria. They were accepted by everyone, but when it came time to write their joint biography towards the end of the century it was necessary to go to great lengths to obscure the fact that they married across racial lines. The new racism had effects everywhere, as did a new Evangelical awakening which released a flood of new recruits who, while often fine missionaries, made local leadership less necessary.

The best-known example concerns the Niger mission. The Church Missionary Society, a Church of England and Evangelical body, had long been under attack from High Churchmen as it worked with virtually no use of bishops in the field. Its talented secretary, Henry Venn, replied that instead of the missionary bishop desired by High Churchmen they preferred the native bishop, though he had to admit that no such person actually existed. In 1864 he arranged that a Yoruba clergyman named Samuel Crowther should be consecrated bishop, originally for the already evangelized portions of what is now Nigeria. This would have been in keeping with the belief that when mission work had reached a certain point, missionaries should then move on to 'regions beyond' and leave behind a church which would be self-governing, self-propagating, and self-supporting. However, those missionaries involved in educational and medical and other works in the parts of Nigeria to be under Crowther's oversight were opposed to the idea, and this is hardly surprising, since Venn's theory only took into account the single missionary work of evangelism and ignored everything else. Venn then stood his own theory on its head and made Crowther a missionary bishop on the upper Niger, with no self-governing church and with all his activities financed from London. He now had a native bishop to show to his critics, though in fact his native bishop was a missionary bishop who happened to be a native.

The next step in the process occurred in Cambridge, where Evangelical students were volunteering for missions, but threatened to desert bodies like the Church Missionary Society in favour of 'faith missions', which expected their staff to live in the faith that God would provide financial support. Two young Cambridge men agreed to serve CMS on the Niger, but depending on what their families and friends might give; they were thus 'honorary' in the eyes of the Society and so not subject to the same discipline as others. On arrival in the field in 1886 they denounced irregularities, and there is no doubt that Crowther had been too willing to think well of his African clergy, who sometimes were not as faultless as he believed. They then removed Bishop Crowther from the finance board of his own mission, and cut off from holy communion nine-tenths of the Christians on the Niger. This was not merely racist, but expressed the new Keswick doctrine of 'holiness'; it is quite possible that these two young men would have done the same thing in England had they had the power to do so. Crowther was old and weak and died shortly afterwards, though his son led a schism which lasted a generation. Meanwhile, the Society in London was disturbed at the action of its two young zealots, and might have finally moved against them had not both died. The situation was stabilized by appointing an English bishop with an African assistant, and by a senior missionary publicly apologizing for the actions of the young zealots at every mission station on the upper Niger. But ultimately no society could move against its home supporters, though it must be admitted that the Church Missionary Society in London made no very strong effort to do so. After the death of Crowther, it took the best part of a century before another African bishop, other than an assistant, was to follow him.

David Livingstone is sometimes considered the typical missionary of his day, yet his popularity may have been due to his not being typical. In the minds of the general public he was a 'good' missionary because he was medical and he was an explorer, and he did not waste his time teaching religion, or if he did do so it was a minor activity. He was thus humanitarian and tolerant, and a rebuke to the religious. In fact his ideas came from the Scotland of his youth. He had the usual Scottish belief in the relics of natural religion from primaeval times, and there is one hilarious incident in which he asks Africans if they have a doctrine of a supreme being, and on being told they do not, asks them if their ancestors did, and is (perhaps in desperation) told that this was the case. He believed that God showed his benevolence in long rivers which allowed trade and civilization, and he found it hard to believe in the existence of waterfalls which denied the benevolence of God, so he imagined rivers to be longer than they really were. He believed that geography was a sacred science intended to guide future missionaries, which thus justified his explorations. As he wrote in 1853, 'Future missionaries will be rewarded by conversions for every sermon. We are their pioneers and helpers. Let them not forget the watchmen of the night . . .' He also believed that the world was 'rolling on to the golden age' with the advance of civilization, and this civilization 'alone produces beauty, and exposure to the weather and other vicissitudes tend to the production of deformation and ugliness . . .' This was linked to his astonishing statement that he had 'never met a beautiful woman among the black people', but towards the end of his days he had to realize that physical beauty and civilization, let alone holiness, were in no way connected. Indeed, Livingstone may be seen as the ideal searcher for knowledge of the eighteenth century, glorifying God in his search, but finally abandoning all such concerns as he gave himself for the lives and the needs of those whom he met in Africa.

There is one thing to be found in almost any missionary history. The mission started in one place, failed to make converts, and moved elsewhere. This means that a mission could only function where a demand for it existed. It could not create that demand. Of course some missions died out before they could move, or failed to find any response even after having moved, but their histories have not been written. We tend to believe that missionaries went out into the world with an aggressive ideology which the poor heathen could not resist. The evidence suggests that the missionary was looking for openings, and if he found none, then the enterprise failed. Of course this view is not popular amongst those who favour views of white superiority, and much modern criticism of missionary effort may well be an attempt to prove that any white man could dominate any group of natives. Yet it is becoming less fashionable to say that Europeans exerted their wills on helpless Africans and Asians; a Nigerian scholar has pointed out that, 'while the lives of some people were completely transformed, others hardly knew the European rulers were here before they began to leave'. And many became Christian without much thought of the European or American missionaries, who were only dimly recognized to have their place somewhere behind the local evangelists who were the people that really mattered. But the last word must be left to Arthur Schlesinger Jr, who has written, 'In his way ... the missionary was an agent of the Western assault on non-Western societies. But his way was not the way laid out in the classical theories of economic and political imperialism.' The missionary took what his home society did not think could or should be taken, and he tried to find somebody who wanted it. Sometimes he succeeded, and sometimes he did not. If in one generation the numbers of African Christians have grown from twenty-five to a hundred million, which is perhaps the most significant fact in all modern church history, in other countries the Christian presence was established in a specific decade, after which the shutters came down and future growth proved impossible. And in some countries many years of missionary work had no effect at all.

13

Fundamentalism

There are two types of wrist-watches. One is the analogue watch, in which small hands turn slowly round and point to numbers. If you have such a watch you know that the position of the hand is not the time of day, but from it you can work out the time of day. The other type of wrist-watch is the digital, in which numbers actually appear on a small screen. Of course people buy different types of wrist-watches for all sorts of reasons, but in theory we should expect those who prefer wrist-watches with turning hands to believe that images or symbols are only distantly related to whatever things we learn from them. On the other hand, we should expect those who prefer wrist-watches with flashing numbers to believe that images or symbols not only point to truths but clearly express those truths.

Fundamentalists believed that words were closely identified with their meanings. 'No man can have a wordless thought', claimed Charles Hodge, one of the founding fathers of the 'Princeton theology' in America. For Hodge, there were no words expressing a thought which lay behind them, but the thought itself was in words, and the words were thoughts. This is probably derived from 'Scottish common-sense philosophy' of the eighteenth century, whereby anyone using his common-sense could understand what any set of words meant, and Scottish common-sense philosophy continued to be strong in America long after it faded in Scotland. So, if you held this philosophy, then the words of the Bible were the Bible itself, and were the message of the Bible. There could not be more than one interpretation of any passage; the passage was the interpretation and the medium was the message.

If the intellectual foundations of Fundamentalism were built upon a certain philosophy, they were also influenced by a particular view of science. Today scientific principles are not as absolute as they were.

They are helpful ways in which to understand what is happening. The old science with its unchanging laws was modified by Max Planck and Einstein and the quantum physicists. The philosopher A. N. Whitehead once wrote of the 'misplaced concreteness' which flowed from science into philosophy; it also flowed into religion, and by treating religion as a set of scientific laws the Fundamentalists made it compatible with science in an age when science seemed the dominant way of thought. In fact, the Fundamentalist outlook may have been necessary as the only Christian outlook possible for those living in a world of old-fashioned science, and if this seems patronizing, then it must be said that most theological systems exist for peoples who have inherited some sort of philosophy and to whom preaching must be done according to that philosophy. Of course it is ironic that a religious system of which its strength was its nearness to a particular view of science should have flourished in the precise years when that view of science was declining, but it is possible that an awareness that their science was being replaced led the Fundamentalists to fight all the harder against a world which had abandoned everything which they believed. It is more ironic that present-day Fundamentalists should have found it necessary to recreate a science which the scientists had abandoned in order to support their religious system. But it can be seen that whatever else may be said of Fundamentalism, it was intellectual in origin. It was not, as has frequently been suggested, just ignorance and emotion.

But something more should be said of the eighteenth-century way of looking at things. It was then assumed that almost everything was done by God at the creation, and all Christian life and revealed truth came from the creation. Somehow a similar view of the Bible seems to have developed: that all divine input or inspiration came when the words were written, and anything done later by editors was not inspired and was, in fact, human meddling with an inspired text. That the oversight of God came way back at the beginning and then stopped dead was a very eighteenth-century idea, and once applied to the Bible, it could not permit any development in the text.

Yet Fundamentalism was not just about the Bible; it has been argued that Fundamentalists needed a literal Bible to defend everything else which was threatened by a new liberalism. In the late nineteenth century liberals, or some of them, expected the kingdom of God to come with better education, health care and democracy. This would rid the Gospels of their 'magical' elements and leave only the ethical message of the Teacher of Galilee. Against this, Fundamentalists felt they needed a literal Bible to prove the old Christian faith, but they had no need to invent a doctrine of the literal Bible. They came by it naturally.

The Fundamentals were defined at a Bible Conference at Niagara in 1895. They were the Inerrancy of the Bible, the Deity of Christ, the Virgin Birth, the Substitutionary Atonement, and the Bodily Second Coming. These five points were then supported by essays, some scholarly and some not, posted free in millions of pamphlets known as *The Fundamentals* to ministers and religious workers between 1906 and 1915. If they converted few, they may have given an illusion of power to those who were already convinced. And when the First World War was promoted as a crusade against German modernist theology, it led some to believe that after victory in the battlefield that theology should be defeated in the schools and churches of America as well.

In 1919 the World's Christian Fundamentals Association was formed at a mass meeting in Philadelphia. Its aim was to fight various forms of infidelity and bring the churches back to the faith, but it also intended to spearhead a new campaign of mass evangelism directed to the millions supposedly driven out of the churches by modernist teaching. In fact such millions did not exist, and it was not a time in which mass evangelism could be expected to work anyway, so little came of this. But right from the start the dominant issue was evolution.

The case against evolution was that it was not scientific fact since it could not be proved; the Fundamentalists were true followers of Bacon in believing that science was facts and not a way of considering facts. If evolution was not fact, then it must be belief, or religion, and the Constitution outlawed teaching religious doctrines in schools. The truth is that evolution as believed by many in those days, but never by Darwin himself, was a principle of life or virtually a religion, so there was some justice in the Fundamentalist complaint. But this whole campaign ended in farce. It was being directed against the teaching of evolution which was science, and not that which was morality. State legislatures were petitioned to end the teaching of evolution but they usually did nothing or only pretended an interest. In 1923 Tennessee passed a law against teaching evolution, but nobody would have heard of it had it not been for a weird trial in Dayton where some local notables thought it would put the town's name on the map. It did. They made out a case against a young man, primarily a football coach, who had taught evolution, or thought he had taught it, and who did not mind being prosecuted. Earnest liberals paid for the eminent criminal lawyer Clarence Darrow to defend him, and earnest conservatives paid for

Williams Jennings Bryan, thrice presidential candidate in times gone by, to be 'friend of the court' and spokesman against evolution. Darrow, through a long hot summer in Dayton, made mincemeat of poor Bryan, who admitted that he did not take all the Bible literally anyway. Probably many of Bryan's fellow-Fundamentalists did not; they were concerned with more serious things. The football coach was found guilty in such a way that the case was bound to be overturned on appeal, Fundamentalists were made to seem ridiculous, and Bryan died suddenly. But it has been suggested that textbook publishers became nervous as a result of this campaign, and omitted evolution just in case.

The campaign to take over the churches was equally unsuccessful. The Fundamentalists genuinely believed that most Christians were on their side, and the few modernists who had manoeuvred themselves to power in the denominations would be easily removed. Accordingly, they demanded adherence to their standards in synods or conventions or assemblies together with the recall of overseas missionaries who would not conform, and a purge of theological seminaries. But it soon became apparent that the bulk of conservatives distrusted Fundamentalist assumptions, and were antagonized by church meetings being turned into violent confrontations. Of course some denominations were too liberal to be seriously troubled by Fundamentalist pressure, and some were too conservative to be threatened by it, but the Northern Baptists were in the middle and suffered much disruption. Eventually the Baptist dislike of creeds and division between Fundamentalist bodies led to their defeat. Amongst the Northern Presbyterians the leading Fundamentalist was J. Gresham Machen, a scholar of note, and the campaign was initially directed at Harry Emerson Fosdick, minister of First Presbyterian Church in New York, though himself a Baptist. Fosdick was strongly anti-Fundamentalist and the sort of liberal whose views would be almost unimaginable today, but at the end of the day he was told to conform to Presbyterian ways or leave. He chose to leave, and a palatial new church was built for him by John D. Rockefeller, who was one of his congregation. But on other issues the Fundamentalists were unsuccessful and the battles of the 1920s left them bruised and beaten.

Yet they bounced back. In 1941 was founded the National Association of Evangelicals, which initially included such Fundamentalists as Bob Jones, together with moderates. In 1947 Fuller Theological Seminary was established to re-fashion Fundamentalism, while that word was quietly dropped. The creed of Fuller was conservative but not narrow;

in due course the books of the Bible were to be 'interpreted according to their context and purpose'. Although Bob Jones and others soon left, the so-called 'New Evangelicals' increased their numbers through the 1950s when evangelism was once more a realistic possibility.

Billy Graham, who started as an ordinary Evangelical and then became a Fundamentalist, had made his name in the Los Angeles crusade of 1949. But in 1954 Graham was in England where he found no rigid division between Fundamentalists and others, and where he could thus enjoy wider support. In his Scottish campaign of 1956 he had difficulty in keeping the trust of his American supporters and also of the Church of Scotland, but he managed to do so. Back home it was not so easy; when he conducted his New York crusade of 1957 he rejected Fundamentalist sponsorship for that of mainstream Protestants, though the decisive break may have occurred in the previous year when he sided with the Southern Baptist Convention, which was conservative enough for most people, against one of their congregations which was even more conservative. With Graham into an intermediate position went most of the former Fundamentalists, leaving a remnant which was increasingly isolated. It has been argued that the New Evangelicals and those who moved with Billy Graham expected that they would soon win the dominance denied to the former Fundamentalists in the 1920s. If they ever had such hopes they were not realized, but the voice of Conservative Evangelicalism was now to be taken seriously. Meanwhile, in the Church of England the Evangelicals had been somewhat irrelevant and ineffectual until a new Evangelicalism, led mainly by John Stott, moved towards the centre with a more Anglican and more sacramental and more socially concerned programme. And if this was the case in America and in England, it was also the case in many another country and many another tradition of Evangelicalism.

Pentecostalism is not Fundamentalism, though most classical Pentecostalists are also Fundamentalists. But the one has been optimistic while the other has been pessimistic. Pentecostalism grew out of the Holiness movement, which taught the 'total sanctification' of John Wesley. Briefly, this was an assertion that Christians could in this life attain to total sanctification and live without sin. In Wesley's teaching this was probably a reply to Calvinism which stressed the inability of man to do anything without grace, and if Calvin was relying on the teachings of St Augustine, Wesley was coming perilously close to the teaching of Augustine's opponent, Pelagius, who gave his name to the heresy of over-optimism about the capacity of mankind for doing good without grace.

But there is further evidence that Pentecostalism is amongst those theological movements which are basically optimistic about mankind. From the earliest days there has been a strand of the movement known as the 'Oneness' or 'Jesus Only' Pentecostalists, who have taught that God is Jesus and there is only one person and no Trinity. This is essentially the Sabellian or Modalist heresy of the early church, which was optimistic about makind, and if 'Oneness' Pentecostalists are perhaps less than a fifth of the total number in America, they are nonetheless an indication of how the movement arose. But it must be asserted that on the Trinity most Pentecostalists are quite orthodox.

In Holiness teaching, both at Keswick in England and also in America, there were stages in Christian development, first justification in the remission of sins, and then sanctification which was not for everybody and not necessary for salvation. Where Holiness shaded over into Pentecostalism, speaking-in-tongues or 'spirit baptism' became a sign of sanctification, and then in most Pentecostalist denominations a replacement for sanctification. This gift of tongues is not given to every Pentecostalist, and the desperate attempts to keep it alive suggest that it may be declining. It is something which most world religions seem to produce for periods in their history. There have been Pentecostalists who have believed that their 'tongues' were real languages, which linguistic study suggests they are not, while other Pentecostalists have seen them as a language of prayer or praise. Pentecostalists rarely distinguish between what is heard in their worship and is also described in First Corinthians, and what is described as having happened at Pentecost. Though the one is not understood by anyone present, and the other was understood by all present, they are seen as essentially the same, and this may come from treating the Bible as a single text with no distinction between sources.

Modern Pentecostalism dates from the work of Charles Parham, who hoped that the language barrier to foreign missions would be overcome by everyone having a gift in some language. In 1900 he laid hands on a woman in Topeka and she spoke what was thought to be Chinese for three days; early in the following year many of Parham's followers spoke what were claimed to be human languages. One of his adherents, William J. Seymour, who had to be instructed in an adjoining room as he was black, went to Los Angeles in 1906. There an eight-year-old boy received baptism of the Holy Spirit, and a former church on Azusa

Street became the centre. A primarily black group became inter-racial, drawing ministers and others from across the country and beyond. It also drew Parham, who was horrified by divisions amongst the faithful, doubted if the speaking was in real languages, and soon left for obscurity. But the Azusa Street revival led to the Assemblies of God, still the major Pentecostalist denomination, which in 1918 made speaking in tongues the only sign of baptism in the Spirit, instead of being one sign amongst many. But it may be that other groups, notably the many ones using the title 'Church of God', and still maintaining the three stages of conversion, santification and Spirit baptism, were actively speaking in tongues long before Azusa Street, and in Britain the various Pentecostal groups which emerged in that era owed more to the Welsh Revival of 1906 than to anything which happened in America.

The spread of Pentecostalism has been erratic. Nobody knows why it has been successful in South Africa but scarcely elsewhere in Africa. Nobody knows why it flourishes in parts of Latin America, but not in Asia. It has even been suggested that speaking in tongues has become a mere trademark, and the real key to the movement is its worship and preaching. In many ways it is a very sacramental movement, extending the ranges of the 1840s stress on the doctrine of the church, and in most countries the eucharist is celebrated weekly. More notably, Pentecostals have a restrained reverence instead of the emotionalism so often ascribed to them. And if they do emphasize the doctrine of the church, it is hardly surprising that they believe themselves to be the church set off from a world given to permissiveness, evolution, and other evils which they have overcome.

Yet their understanding of themselves has been threatened by the growth of 'charismatics' or Neo-Pentecostalists in the mainline churches. At first the classic Pentecostalists thought that the Neo-Pentecostalists might join them, but when they stayed where they were this made nonsense of the classic Pentecostalist belief that only *their* churches were true, and the others lost to Modernism. There were some attempts at reconciliation, and yet in the long run the two movements went their separate ways.

Charismatics in the mainline churches began in the 1950s, usually in wealthy suburbs or university communities. American beginnings were partly in California and partly in Pennsylvania, where Roman Catholics drew from Protestant experience. However, the best-known group of Catholic charismatics derived from Cursillo, a Hispanic programme for short retreats, which entered the United States from Mexico in 1958 and was initially alien to a largely Irish-dominated church. And Catholic charismatics have always been more guarded than Protestants in their view of speaking in tongues, which is seen more as a language of prayer than a baptism of the Spirit. In Britain the charismatics grew up in the Evangelical wing of the Church of England, where there was some opposition to what appeared to be revelation subsequent to Scripture. Yet there has been a surprising tolerance of charismatics in all demoninations, derived as much from an inability to do anything about them as from a desire to keep them in the fold if at all possible. And the charismatics have usually acted to prevent division in the churches, while with their music they have enriched church life beyond their own sympathizers.

Yet if speaking in tongues amongst the charismatics is not connected with nineteenth-century Holiness, it is harder to say just why it arose. The most convincing suggestion is that it was an outcome of the antiverbal climate of the 1960s, when words were believed to obscure truths rather than proclaim them, and this philosophy might well have led to a religious movement avoiding words in the deeper moments of prayer. The movement certainly flourished amongst those social classes who were most receptive to the ideas of the 1960s and placed most emphasis on 'personal development'. This raises another question: does the emphasis of the charismatics on their own happiness justify accusations of self-indulgence? And if the classic Pentecostalists are to be considered, after three-quarters of a century they have done virtually nothing in works of mercy, though many of them are reasonably affluent, and they have made no noteworthy impression in missions to those outside Christianity. Perhaps the truth is that if Christians enjoy heavenly blessings as a major part of their religious life, the world which is around them may be considered to be part of the past, and unworthy of their attention. But amongst both classical Pentecostalists and charismatics there are so many men and women of good-will and compassion that their lack of corporate expression of that compassion must be attributed to some deep conviction and not to self-interest.

Lastly, there is a parallel between Pentecostalism amongst Protestants and devotion to the Blessed Virgin Mary amongst Roman Catholics. The doctrine of the Immaculate Conception, declared to be an essential part of the Catholic faith in 1854, held that Mary was conceived without sin, and this is essentially the same thing as total sanctification. It holds that one person could and did live without sin, and this allowed the degree of free will necessary for her to accept the destiny announced by the angel Gabriel. Without this it might be implied that salvation could not be accomplished as human participation was unwilling, but only in a time when human participation was considered necessary would such an argument be advanced. Subsequent developments of Marian devotion, including places of healing, can be compared to heavenly gifts amongst Pentecostals. The conclusion to be reached is that the theological basis for both movements were the same, though their development was different.

14

The Soviet Union

It is tempting for Christians in the West to use church life in the Soviet Union to prove some theory about church life in their own lands. That there is a battle between rival ideologies, it being presumed that the Soviet authorities think that Christianity is an ideology in the same sense as is Marxism. That there is in the Soviet Union a true church which is persecuted and a false church which is favoured by authority, this being how they regard the religious bodies of the West. That moral choices for Christians in the Soviet Union are clear, so that heroes and villains can be easily distinguished. That persecution is good for a church and produces a purer Christianity than does tolerance. These views and many others like them overlook the fact that the Soviet Union is a real country, or a real group of countries, and its people are real people and not just figments of our imagination.

One of the great calamities of Russian history was the triumph of Poland in the sixteenth century, with Polish rule extending almost to the Black Sea. In 1596 the Unia (union) of Brest-Litovsk placed the Orthodox church of the Ukraine, south of Russia proper, under the Pope, though leaving it with a married clergy and an Eastern liturgy. This was to be the pattern for all 'Uniat' churches in the future; segments of Orthodox bodies which accepted the Papacy, and were regarded with horror by the uncorrupted Orthodox. Over the next two centuries the Russians pushed the Poles and their Lithuanian allies back, and with Prussia and Austria they eventually eliminated the Polish state, but they did not eliminate the Uniat church. Catherine the Great did her best or worst; she cut their numbers from ten to two million. By 1875 the Uniat church was only legal in Austrian territory, while in Russian territory the Latin-rite Catholics were also persecuted and in many areas disappeared. But after the 1905 uprising came a relaxation of oppression, and both Latins and Uniats increased. Yet in the eyes of true Russians they were part of a great plot to undermine Russian nationality and culture, for the Poles had betrayed the Slavic family by their Roman Catholicism, while the Ukrainians had done likewise by clinging to their connection with Rome. That connection was a rebuke to Russian Orthodoxy, and also a threat to Moscow rule, whether imperial or Marxist. When the Russian Patriarchate was proclaimed in 1589, and the idea of Moscow as a 'Third Rome' was openly set forth, it was partly with the aim of holding back the Latin threat. Ever since, there has been a fear of Ukrainian nationalism seen in religious terms.

Between the February Revolution of 1917 and the 'Bolshevik' Revolution in October of that year, the Russian Orthodox Church was reformed according to plans drawn up for 1905 but abandoned when state oppression was reimposed. The Patriarchate, abolished by Peter the Great as an obstacle to state control, was recreated and filled by Tikhon, formerly bishop in San Francisco and thus accustomed to secular rule. Two days later the Bolsheviks seized Moscow and the Civil War divided the church, and yet the Patriarchate survived. In the south there was a group of bishops under monarchisat rule who were eventually driven into exile, but there was also a Ukrainian Autocephalous Church. Since there were no Ukrainians as bishops under the old regime, they resorted to the consecration of bishops by priests, and had various doctrinal irregularities as well. This body was quickly suppressed by the Red Army, only to reappear in the Second World War. And in Russia itself there was a 'Living Church', very much a Soviet creation to undermine the bishops. The idea was to divide and rule, and in a sense this served the church, which always had a variety of centres, one of which was sure to be appropriate to whatever the political outcome of the Civil War might be.

The Patriarchate proved to be the centre which survived. Tikhon did excommunicate the Bolshevik leaders, but he did not support the monarchist armies, and he did not reject the civil authority of the Marxist state. In fact he was too accommodating for some, and this led to the Josephite schism which lingered on as another option even if its hour never came. In 1922 Tikhon was imprisoned on cleverly arranged charges linked to famine relief; on his release he was more conciliatory, though he did denounce the Living Church movement. On his death in 1925 he left a list of three successors, since election was impossible. All chanced to be in prison, but Sergius, who was on one of *their* lists, assumed the leadership. He had been a missionary in Japan, a chaplain in Athens and a bishop of Finland, and was thus familiar with various forms of church-state relationships, though he had seen nothing, and history had seen nothing, of persecution such as that to be unleashed in the Soviet Union.

Sergius co-operated with the state to save the church. He demanded that all Russian clergy, at home or abroad, should take an oath of loyalty to the Soviet regime, which lost him the allegiance of his over-seas following, who placed themselves under either Constantinople or a new American jurisdiction. Yet it may have enabled the church to hang on until things changed. In 1917 there had been 270 bishops; by 1939 only six or seven were in their dioceses. Twelve thousand clergy are estimated to have been executed or to have died in camps where the diet was such as to leave inmates too weak to resist any illness. And it must be added that there were some Russians who were not Marxists but saw religion as an aid to superstition and a bar to progress; a parallel has even been drawn between the American attempt to outlaw alcohol and the Soviet attempt to outlaw religion. Yet the persecution was never absolute, and it usually occurred when there was some assumed threat and churchmen were thought to be potential allies to more dangerous forces. First in the Civil War, then with the campaign against the peasants, then in the great purges of supposed spies and traitors, per-secutions mounted in intensity, but at no time was there a policy to destroy the church completely. This might have been done had there been a will to do it, but the Soviets saw no need for such a policy. In their view religion was only a shadow of economic circumstances, and when these changed, religion would disappear. And they preferred to have a visible church instead of underground movements which they could not monitor. Furthermore, they saw the church as useful in influencing foreign opinion, and since Marxists believe that churches exist to influence opinion, they exaggerate its effectiveness in so doing. As for religious groups not centred on Moscow, they treated these as foreign agencies and the small Protestant groups were largely destroyed, while the vast majority of Roman Catholic and Uniat priests were imprisoned or executed.

Yet it would be wrong to think that the Soviet leadership saw them-selves as engaged in a battle with Christianity. Christians tend to think that only Christians suffered, and Jews tend to think that only Jews suffered, and so on. But everybody suffered. Christians, Jews, Muslims, peasants, workers, geneticists, economists, until eventually Stalin devoted himself to killing off the old Bolsheviks. Christians were largely incidental, though naturally they did not see their sufferings in that light.

War changed the picture. The church became a useful, or an apparently useful, means of controlling the population. And there were new populations to control, for in 1939 the Soviets took half Poland while the Nazis took the other half, and in 1940 the Soviets annexed the three Baltic republics and much of Romania. There was no time to subdue these peoples; that would come after 1945. But in the meantime churches could be used for the 'social control' which Marxists believed to be their main function, and they were so used. Three of the few bishops left to the Russian Orthodox Church were shipped to the newly occupied territories to bring the churches there under Moscow or, in the minds of the bishops, to provide a shield from Moscow by convincing the authorities that the churches served Moscow. But it was not only the Orthodox who provided this service to the Kremlin; two Baptist leaders were sent to the Baltic states to influence Protestants there. And as long as churches were being presented to new populations as true churches, they had to be given at least some appearance of normal church life, and persecution began to slacken.

In 1941 the Nazis invaded the Soviet Union. For three years they occupied vast areas of Soviet territory, and while their rule was in everything else less welcome than that of the Soviets, they did allow churches to reopen. German military chaplains were often the leaders in this, while German agencies other than the army frowned on any religious activity amongst what they regarded as underpeople, though if they found it they tried to use it. The classic case is that of Sergius, called the 'younger' to distinguish him from the bishop of Moscow. He had been one of the three bishops sent to the West in 1940, in his case to Riga in Latvia, where he was initially distrusted by the Paris-trained clergy who had seen their beloved bishop shipped off to oblivion and this Moscow tough imposed upon them. When the German armies arrived in 1941 he was ordered to retreat with the Red Army, but hid in the cathedral crypt and emerged to welcome the Germans as liberators. When some of his clergy expressed pessimism he told them that if they had had experience in fooling the security men in Moscow, then they would have thought nothing of deceiving the Germans. From his base in the Baltic republics he sent priests eastward behind the ranks of the advancing German army to Pskov in Russia, opening churches, ordaining new priests, and starting a widespread religious revival. Yet he did not live to see the results. He was murdered either by the Germans or the

Soviets, and it does not really matter which. He had done what was necessary.

When it had become known that the Germans were welcomed as liberators in the Ukraine, and sometimes elsewhere, the Soviets responded by allowing churches to reopen in areas as yet unoccupied. Sergius of Moscow was one of the notables evacuated from the city when it was expected to fall to the German armies, and in 1944 he was formally elected Patriarch, though those bishops sent to Moscow to elect him would have been outnumbered by the bishops still in prison. But gradually bishops and priests were released, and new ones consecrated and ordained. By 1942 there were eleven bishops, by 1945 there were forty-six, and by 1949 there were seventy-four.

But there were complications in the Ukraine. There were the Orthodox under Moscow, those 'autocephalous' Orthodox who were independent and nationalist, and the Uniats under Rome. The first two groups had a thousand priests between them by 1943, two-thirds the number that there had been in 1917. There were moves for union between them, but the leaders of both groups were assassinated. When the Red Army reoccupied the Ukraine the bishops of the independent church mainly fled to the West, while most of the Moscow bishops were sent to Siberia. As for the Uniats, they were almost totally absorbed into the Russian Orthodox Church after a puppet council of a few rebel clergy voted for this, and the eight hundred priests who resisted disappeared into labour camps. The future pattern was to be controlled Orthodoxy within the Soviet Union, and tolerated Catholicism within Eastern Europe, Catholic Lithuania being the exception. The border with Poland roughly followed religious lines. It was estimated that before the change of policy in 1959 there were about twenty thousand churches open in the Soviet Union, with about thirty million regular worshippers. Significantly, open churches were mainly to be found in the south and west where Ukrainian religious nationalism might be a danger if no churches were open. As for those who attend worship, they have tended to be divided between the uneducated masses and the intellectuals, but not those in between, which is utterly contrary to the experience of the churches in the West. On the other hand skilled workers and clerks and managers, who are the backbone of church life in Britain or America, tend to be moved to activism rather than contemplation, and find the Orthodox liturgy boring and meaningless. They are more likely to feel at home with the Baptists, if they are attracted to religion at all.

After the Second World War it might have seemed that Stalin would persecute the churches again, but this did not happen. Possibly this was because Stalin had more important things to do and restructing industry took priority over crushing religion, which was considered to be something for peasants. On the other hand, Stalin is said to have built up the Communist Party rapidly after its wartime decline to offset the army and the industrialists, so the church may have seemed to him to be a useful counterweight to one potential enemy or another.

But all changed with the coming to power of Khrushchev. Stalin's reign of terror ended, though more subtle forms of repression did not. And yet an easing of restrictions in all other fields was accompanied by renewed harassment of religion. Between 1959 and 1964 half the churches were closed and about two-thirds of the Orthodox clergy forced to abandon their ministry or continue it illegally. In 1961 a synod of the bishops was required to agree to new rules which gave effective control of each parish church to a committee which could be dominated by unbelievers or those who wasted church funds. Only acts of worship were left to the clergy.

Why Khrushchev should have taken this action has never been clear, but it probably had something to do with his agricultural policy. His aim was to bring the despised peasants into the mainstream of Soviet life, and this meant delivering them, in the most humanitarian way, from the grip of superstition. As full Soviet citizens they would no longer need social control through religion, and they would also become more productive. In fact they did not, and critics have grumbled that Khrushchev drove the peasants off the land by his anti-religious measures. But when Khrushchev fell from power the restrictions of his rule were allowed to remain, though they were not taken further. The whole subject of religion was left in mid-air.

A word must be said of Evangelicals, which is the title usually given to the various groups of Protestants. Numerically these groups are very limited in comparison with the Orthodox, and yet their response to state pressures has been very similar. There are two historic groups, Baptists and Evangelical Christians, the latter being somewhat like Presbyterians but with little doctrine of ministry and somewhat nearer to the Brethren in the West. Having suffered much in the days of imperial rule, they welcomed new opportunities both in 1905 and in 1917, but speedily came under attack from the Bolsheviks, as did the Mennonites whose pacifism made them a particular target. A projected union in 1925 came to nothing, but in the Second World War the Soviet authorities decided to take them in hand, much as they did the Orthodox, and the result was a forced union in 1944. This was dominated by the Evangelical Christians, though on the subjects of sacraments and ministry the stricter Baptist views were accepted. After the war the Evangelical Christian majority was offset by the Baptists, three-quarters of whom were in former Polish or Romanian territory. Pentecostalists were also brought into this union, though since all their Pentecostalist activities were forbidden they either left the union or ceased to be Pentecostalist. Of one leader from that period it has been written by Walter Sawatsky, 'Perhaps he had experienced especially severe prison conditions, perhaps he was especially susceptible to pain, perhaps the authorities were able to blackmail him, perhaps he truly felt that Romans 13 demanded full submission to state authorities', and it is difficult for us to judge such people. In 1961 the new harshness of state policy led the leaders of the union to forbid evangelism in order to permit survival until better times, but this led, with similar moves to avoid confrontation, to a revolt of some Baptists who formed a rival organization. The mere existence of such a revolt allowed the majority group, who still had a quarter of a million followers, to retreat from the decrees of 1961. Which group should be regarded as true and which as false is not a very useful question for outsiders. There are times to collaborate, and times to refuse, and those in the Soviet Union must make their decisions in the light of their own situation. As for the unregistered or 'Reform' Baptists, they have declined as their membership has returned to the main body, and they have at times found it imprudent to speak of the persecution they have received, as they themselves have sought state recognition. Without state recognition, any form of continuing church life is virtually impossible, and this has meant that difficult moral crises have arisen for absolutely everyone.

This raises a question mentioned at the beginning of this chapter. Is persecution good for a church? Does it lead to growth? Does the blood of the martyrs become the seed of the church? The answer to this question must be a resounding no. Mild and temporary persecution may lead to a feeling of community amongst Christians, but real persecution, in any age, leads to division, denial of Christianity, and mutual suspicion amongst Christians. And this is hardly surprising. If God's plan for the church favoured torture and deprivation for those he loved, then he would hardly be a God of love and his call to follow him would be an invitation into a trap. Persecution may come, but not by his will.

In recent years the situation has changed again. The Gorbachev era has brought 'Glasnost' or openness to religious as well as to secular life, and there are signs of a new freedom. Yet the freedom so far granted to religious believers has been carefully limited and has been most evident in areas of high visibility. Furthermore, there is a sense in which devoted Marxists must reduce religion and its place in everyday life, while cynical tyrants may tolerate and use it. It remains to be seen whether the Soviet state will gradually relax its grip on religion or whether it will embark on a new and less brutal campaign to remove it once and for all.

15

Ecumenism

In 1942 William Temple, Archbishop of Canterbury, said that the ecumenical nature of the church was 'the great new fact of our time'. He did not use the word 'ecumenical' to mean inter-denominational or leading to church union, but rather to mean world-wide instead of being confined to Europe and America. Yet the word has now come to mean world-wide in the sense of inter-church, and if that is not the great new fact of our time, it is still a new fact of our time or, more accurately, of his.

The ecumenical movement developed when it did because of the emphasis on the doctrine of the church in the nineteenth century. Once the church was seen as the mystical body of Christ and not just as a useful bit of machinery, it mattered if it was divided. There were two answers to the problem of a divided church. The first was to insist that it was not divided, since your own part was the true church and the others were not part of the church at all. Before the 1840s there was a good deal of mutual toleration between Christians of different demoninations, but after that period this became rarer. This was not because Christians became nastier than they used to be, but because they had a new problem in combining Christ's prayer for a single church with a practical situation of many churches. The second answer was to try and reunite the various fragments of what was seen to be one church. And yet there were other motives, as there always are, and most of these were practical. Some wanted unity to make social action more effective. Others wanted it to make evangelism more effective. Some merely wanted to make religion cheaper. Many wanted church union because they did not understand the issues and so thought that there were no issues. But others believed that the unity of the church was the will of God, and struggled to move churches closer together while respecting the convictions of those with whom they disagreed.

One early movement for church union was Federationism. This was mainly American, and the first local Federation of Churches was formed at New York in 1880. The aim was to form local federations, state federations, and finally a Federal Council for the entire country. Federations would concern themselves with social service and evangelism, leaving theological and churchly affairs to the denominations, which would gradually fade away as these concerns were seen to be unimportant. Of course this scheme ignored conservative Christians, and anyone at all who was not Protestant, but it was rather vaguely assumed that more education and democracy would wipe out such people anyway. But doctrine proved stronger than supposed, and it was Federationism which withered away, though the Federal Council, now known as the National Council, has survived as a useful body without anyone remembering how it came by its original name. In Britain there was a more scholarly version of Federationism which led to a Federal Council of Evangelical Free Churches in 1916. This was to have been the first step on the way to a wider federation, though it proved to be the last step.

If Federationism was virtually dead by 1920, it had served one purpose. It had scared conservatives out of their wits. They became convinced that union was inevitable, and unless they could find a better way of arranging it, union would be at the expense of faith and order. So they founded a movement for Faith and Order.

The other main movement for church union arose in Evangelicalism but did not stay there. Evangelicals could usually, though not always, move across denominational boundaries while creating rigid walls between themselves and non-Evangelicals. And they believed that faith mattered, even if they were not always sure about order. And they were anxious about the rising generation of leaders in church and state, so in 1862 they founded a Christian Union at Cambridge, with similar bodies elsewhere a few years later. These unions were supposed to be alternatives to the debating unions which prepared young men for parliamentary careers; Christian Unions would prepare them for careers in service to Christ. In America something similar was done within the framework of the student YMCA, which became associated with overseas missions. In 1895 John R. Mott was recruited to lead this movement internationally, and by the following year their slogan was 'the evangelization of the world in this generation'. Whether this meant the conversion of the world, or merely preaching to all the peoples of the world, it was still a breath-taking alliance of traditional Evangelicalism and popular optimism. Meanwhile in Britain the Student Christian Movement, as it was

now called, tried to bring in Christian students who were not actually
Evangelical, and in deference to Anglican order even abandoned its
non-denominational communion services. But once it had become part
of a world fellowship with many non-Evangelicals, the SCM could no
longer maintain the loyalty of its Evangelical founders.

The break came in 1910. The Cambridge Inter-Collegiate Christian
Union withdrew from the national SCM rather than see the Cambridge
Nonconformist Society admitted to the SCM. There may well have
been class overtones in that summer when the landed gentry of England
were under threat from a budget which was to limit their wealth and
their power, but the break was probably inevitable anyway. Ecumenism
and Evangelicalism were now apart, and a new student movement, using
the tradename 'Inter', came into being for true Evangelicals. Meanwhile,
those who had been through the SCM in their youth became leaders of
ecumenism in the various churches, though it is not true that they laid
the groundwork for union in the churches overseas. Few men from the
SCM now went overseas, and the ones selected for India, where union
was already being planned and personnel selected accordingly, were the
exceptions.

In 1910 there also occurred the World Missionary Conference at
Edinburgh. It is sometimes suggested that this brought together world
leaders of missions and thus began the ecumenical movement, but this
would be going too far. What it did do was to provide a structure for
missionary co-operation, which was already long established. From this
Conference came the International Missionary Council which eventually joined the World Council of Churches in 1961, thirteen years after
the latter was formed. It has been claimed that ecumenism was linked
with mission, but if there was a theological truth to this statement it is
more doubtful as an historical claim. The point about the mission field
was that sending churches could mould the shape of missions in a particular area by a careful choice of missionaries, which could not easily
be done at home; that missions tended to be all of one outlook was
largely divorced from expectations of union and stemmed rather from
the origin of missions in societies and not in sending churches. But even
this policy had its limits: if church union depended on missionaries then
the whole programme would fall apart, and sometimes did fall apart
when power was handed over to local leaders who had other priorities.
But this raises another point. There is a story of an old ecumenical war-
horse carefully enlisting 'the people who mattered', and this movement
came into being when it was taken for granted that elites mattered in

every walk of life, and always would. If you caught the leaders in the universities, then all else would follow automatically. To some extent this did work in the early days, but as society changed and as churches changed the ecumenical elite became less and less effective.

But there was another notion at large in this movement which made it seem more suitable for mission churches. This was that the early life of any church was spent in a childish phase of non-denominational Christianity. Such a thing as non-denominational Christianity may be impossible anyway, but the idea is derived from theories about the history of the early church, which supposed that there was a time before that church had serious ideas about anything. If this had once been true, then it would make sense to try and create unions in countries where the church was still at a pre-thinking stage. But in real life even the youngest churches have proved to hold quite sophisticated theological ideas, and younger churches are sometimes more firmly committed to the only form of Christianity which they have known than are older churches with a greater variety in their remembered past.

While the British were forming their ecumenical elite, the American opponents of Federationism called on their European counterparts to join them in a world conference on Faith and Order. War postponed this conference, which did not meet until 1927, but it was this branch of ecumenism which was most concerned with the mechanics of church union. If it tended to belittle differences between churches by calling them 'traditions' as if they were not actual convictions of living people, it was at least anxious to study those differences. But in addition to Faith and Order there was another movement, known as Life and Work, which held its world conference at Stockholm in 1925. There were some who believed that in their life and their work churches were all much the same, and that by concentrating on life and work the difficulties of faith and of order might be put in their place. And yet the concentration of the movement on social problems did lead to a deeper understanding of the Christian faith in a fallen world.

If Life and Work joined with Faith and Order to produce the World Council of Churches in 1948, the actual church unions did not wait for that event. There were a number of unions between the wars, though mostly within denominations which had divided over issues no longer regarded as serious, but these unions would probably have occurred even had there been no ecumenical movement. Methodists rejoined in Britain and in America, and Presbyterians rejoined in Scotland, and in India Congregationalists joined with Presbyterians. There were somewhat wider unions in Japan and in China; that in Japan was enlarged during the war years by government lumping all Protestant churches together, though after the war some churches broke free of that union. In China the onset of Communist rule led to persecution and a 'patriotic' form of Roman Catholicism divorced from Rome was used as a means of control but also served as a means of survival. On the Protestant side all bodies were absorbed into the 'Three-Self Movement', which took its name from the old missionary aim of self-government, self-support, and self-extension. Yet the Three-Self Movement expressed a particular form of Christian life which owed more to the YMCA than to any particular church, and there is a sense in which the YMCA was more at home in China than any Protestant denomination. More closely inspired by the aims of world ecumenism was the formation of the United Church of Canada in 1925, comprising a fifth of the population of that country, and taking in all Methodists and Congregationalists with two-thirds of the Presbyterians. At the time the United Church was presented as something essentially Canadian, and those who stayed out were regarded as relics of Scottish or other national churches, but subsequent study has produced a theory that the United Church was attempting to be a national church such as the Church of Scotland, while the continuing Presbyterians stood for the religious pluralism of the North American scene.

But the union which was to have been an example to all was that of South India. Nearly thirty years in the making, it finally took place in 1947 and brought together over a million Christians who had been Anglicans, Methodists, and members of the older union of Presbyterians and Congregationalists. That it was confined to the south, where most of the Christians of India were found, meant that it was confined to groups with a common British liberal Evangelicalism. There were virtually none who opted out except for a small body of Anglicans who, significantly, were not of Evangelical tradition. That the union was so successful was largely due to its straight-forward nature, and to local church life being left very much as it had been before. Since the union included Anglicans with clergy ordained by bishops, and others ordained by presbyters, and since Anglicans (admittedly not as many in South India as elsewhere) could not recognize clergy not ordained by bishops, the ministry was a key question. The answer was to leave all ministers as they were, though additional bishops were chosen from the various participating churches and then consecrated, with future ordinations to be by bishops with presbyters participating. A conscience clause protected any congregation which had doubts about the ordination of any minister, but after a generation there were hardly any ministers whose ordination was not acceptable to all. With hindsight the Church of South India would seem to have been a model union, and if it was untidy to have a church with ministers of various ordinations, that was still better than having those same ministers in different churches.

Yet that union created an uproar in the Church of England for reasons which are still unclear. Few in that church had taken much interest in the overseas field before this. It is possible that after political withdrawal from India had led to massacre and a feeling in Britain that people had been abandoned, there was a feeling amongst churchmen that Anglicans in India were also being abandoned. But if there was extraordinary agitation because the union in South India went too far, some of the same protesters claimed that it did not go far enough. It did not provide a ministry universally recognized in India, let alone overseas. Thus it seemed that the way to answer these criticisms was to arrange that future unions should have unified ministries from the very beginning. This would allow them to be recognized by the Church of England, though perhaps this was not as important as it seemed at the time.

There was a theology available for this. It went back to the 1920s, and the idea that authority in the church varies in effectiveness according to the proportion of the world's Christians behind each ordination. If this were accepted, then all ordinations were imperfect, and each denomination had something to give to ministers of other denominations in an act of union. This would justify a ceremony remarkably like an ordination, which Anglicans could regard as an ordination, but which non-Anglicans could deny was any such thing. Unhappily this approach depended on a theology which was already in decline, and it was particularly unpopular with precisely those Anglicans whom it was intended to pacify. But it is probably true to say that schemes of this nature were only introduced at such a late date that a change in the theological climate nipped them in the bud. The scheme in Nigeria might have coasted to success with the momentum of earlier days, but a law-suit by Methodists called for a halt when the stadium was already booked for the ceremony of unification. It was recognized that once that moment had passed, there was no hope of rekindling enthusiasm for another attempt. Only in North India, Sri Lanka and Pakistan, where plans laid in earlier days were still forceful enough to bring about unions in 1970, did ceremonies for unifying ministries actually receive a trial. In England the ceremony between Methodists and Anglicans was to be called an Act of

Reconciliation, as if clergy of those two churches had been actively snarling at each other, but the scheme fell through and nothing happened. And yet it was not clear why nothing happened in that case. The Church of England did not produce the expected support for the scheme, but this still does not answer the key question: did the Church of England reject its ecumenical elite because it was ecumenical or because it was an elite?

But everything fell through. Everywhere ecumenism was loud with the noise of nothing happening. Schemes of Covenant, whereby churches solemnly swore that they would unite, did not in fact bring them to unite. There was a successful union of Methodists, Presbyterians and Congregationalists in Australia, but that only did what others had done a generation earlier. The ecumenical movement was over. And the reason that it was over was that the theological stress on the importance of the church which came from the 1840s was no longer there. The cultural firestorm of the 1960s had centred on the rejection of institutions and of intermediate agencies between the observer and reality. That meant the church was no longer the chosen way to God but a barrier between us and God. It was now a positive virtue to ignore institutions, and to ignore the church. And yet there was a growth of fellowship between Christians which resulted, paradoxically, from exactly that factor which had scuttled ecumenism. If the church was now unimportant, it did not matter if Christians belonged to different churches, and they could all be happy together, Roman Catholics included, and indeed it was not long before they called this mutual happiness by the word 'ecumenism'. Going further, they even described it as true ecumenism and took great pleasure in pointing out that they did not believe in 'ecclesiastical joinery'. Against this, it might have been argued that the church was the work of a Carpenter in the first place, and those who followed him had a duty to use hammer and saw to make his work fit his will, but the climate was against such a reply.

Yet there was unfinished business after the collapse. There was the World Council of Churches which had its roots in the graveyard of Federationism, though it was not so much intended to replace the denominations as to bring into being the 'coming great church' and then, presumably, fade away itself. The torrent of paper which came from the World Council, and was not even halted by the computer age, said very little about the ultimate fate intended for that body. In fact there was no need to decide anything as long as church union was postponed indefinitely, and yet Christians wished to work together and needed an instrument through which to work. Nobody proposed to abolish the World Council, though there was constant grumbling about some of its activities, and though the presence of Roman Catholics in world ecumenism but not in the World Council made that body seem somewhat provincial. It was constantly said that Roman Catholics would eventually join, but even in the less churchly atmosphere of the late twentieth century they could hardly feel at home in a body which had Protestant values so deep in its soul. Orthodox participation had always been a sign of comprehension rather than a serious influence on the workings of the Council, and the presence of the Russian Orthodox seemed to be largely intended to prevent the Council working to the detriment of the Soviet state, though Russian churchmen could hardly have been blamed for taking this chance to show Soviet officials how highly they were regarded abroad, and world ecumenists could hardly be blamed for going along with the charade in order to protect Christianity in the Soviet Union. Yet all in all the Orthodox example was not reassuring for Roman Catholics.

But the main unfinished business was ecumenism itself. That one ecumenical movement was over did not mean that there would not be another, and perhaps another and another after that. Divisions in the church have always existed, and there have always been occasions when it has been necessary for somebody, somewhere, to leave and to set up a rival body. Yet in time the reasons for the divisions become less pressing, or are overcome by new developments, and it is possible to put back together the fragments of an earlier age. In some climates of opinion this is made easy and in others it is made difficult, but it can be done, and in church history it is always being done. Ecumenism is not over, though one particular movement may be.

16

The Vatican Councils

For better or worse, Christianity is mainly Roman Catholic. And, also for better or worse, Roman Catholicism undergoes the same processes as other Christian bodies at the same times, though not in quite the same ways. It is as if a wave swept across the sea, raising various pieces of flotsame at some distances from each other, then letting them fall again. And Roman Catholicism bobs up and down far more readily than most other forms of Christianity; they are half-waterlogged by comparison. That Rome is conservative and slow may be true, but Roman Catholicism is not. It may be the effect of a celibate clergy who are able to manoeuvre in and out of new ways of thought without being too involved in family cares, or it may be the effect of vast numbers of followers who cannot be held back by authority. But the result is the same – Roman Catholicism has a tendency to go to extremes.

The first Vatican Council of 1869–70 was the one that defined the infallibility of the Pope. That was pretty extreme, though the actual definition was carefully guarded. But what happened then was happening everywhere. It was not, as so many Protestants have argued, a purely Roman thing at one end of the spectrum, with Protestants being at the other. They had their own versions of the same thing, though their water-logged state made it less perilous. But it was perhaps not so much one thing as two things. The first was the 'two kingdoms' teaching of the 1840s, in which churchmen demanded spiritual independence, and this was found almost everywhere. It caused churches to collide with states just when states were taking aboard extreme claims of state authority over everything. This could be seen in the Church of England, in the Disruption of the Church of Scotland, in American debates over slavery, in Russian Orthodoxy, in France, in Germany, and above all in Rome's determination not to be merely Italian. The Roman definition of church authority was more far-reaching than definitions by other churches, but they all belonged to the same trend.

On the same subject, there was also a tendency for churches to give ultimate authority to central bodies, just as was done by secular governments. It was in the same decade as the first Vatican Council that the Free Church of Scotland, that most un-Roman body, affirmed that it had a *nobile officium* or 'reserve of powers' in its General Assembly which permitted that organ to do anything not specifically reserved to presbyteries. Lastly, it cannot be entirely coincidental that the infallibility of the Pope and the infallibility of Scripture were defined at about the same time in quite different places and circumstances.

The second wave which had the misfortune to coincide with the first concerned choice. In the latter part of the nineteenth century there was an emphasis on choosing, voting, making decisions, and on who chose or made decisions. If Moody called on people to make a decision for Christ and if congregations sang, 'Once to every man and nation, Comes the moment to decide . . .', then it mattered who made ultimate decisions, and this was expecially so around 1870.

Vatican One, as the first council is usually called, was never intended to deal with infallibility. It was planned years earlier to reform the church and to reunite Christians, which was roughly the aim of Vatican Two. But if Vatican Two at least did some of what it was supposed to do, Vatican One did not. It was side-tracked on to the subject of infallibility.

Ecumenical Councils are councils of bishops, with a few others. Non-Catholics were also invited, but not as observers; they were to be penitents seeking forgiveness and readmission. Protestants were crassly invited to return to Rome 'in view of the innumerable sects into which Protestantism has broken up', and the Orthodox were not treated much better. All declined, and all were forgotten by those who assembled. Catholic sovereigns were entitled to attend, except the King of Italy who was excommunicate for seeking to take over the Papal States, but none wanted to attend and none were really welcome anyway. Their presence would have undermined the image of the church as a totally non-state body.

On 2 December 1869 some 43 cardinals, 605 bishops, 31 abbots or equivalents, and a few others, met in a hall which prevented anyone hearing very much. Serious debate began in January, and to the surprise of many, the bishops were intensely critical of the documents they were called to discuss. They found them woolly and outdated. They demanded rewriting, which was done, and Council members worked on

until March, making good progress, though even in a different hall they
found it hard to hear what was said. But the work they did was of little
interest to most Catholics, who knew nothing of what was happening
anyway. What most Catholics did know about was infallibility, and what
they expected was a decree on infallibility. There was a good case for
postponing the issues of faith and structure until the popular matter of
infallibility was out of the way.

Some bishops were anxious that it should be defined by the Council.
Cardinal Manning of England held that it would attract Protestant converts seeking certainty, and Cardinal Cullen of Dublin was almost as
enthusiastic, while the Archbishop of Malines in Belgium was the effective leader of those who wanted the belief to become a required doctrine.
Bishops from Italy and Spain wanted it for devotional reasons, as did
some of the French, who were most violent on both sides of the argument. Against the adherents of the decree were a number of bishops who
believed in infallibility but held it to be 'inopportune' to define it and
thus create opposition. Many of these were French, but some were
German or Austrian bishops who had just had troubles with their
governments and wanted to avoid more troubles. On the other hand,
some accepted infallibility of the Pope but wished it to be infallibility of
Pope and bishops working together, and some feared wild extensions of
infallibility into everyday life. They particularly distrusted French zealots who said that if the Pope were declared infallible then councils
would be unnecessary, and there was even one Englishman who wanted
an infallible Papal bull every morning at breakfast with his copy of *The
Times*.

A petition of bishops requesting that the 'question' be put was duly
considered and approved. And it may well be that many bishops, after
wrestling over difficult questions in debate, welcomed something more
purely theological. They certainly debated infallibility at length, thirty-
nine speaking for it and twenty-six speaking against it. Discussion
closed on 4 July, and there was a trial ballot on 13 July which found 451
in favour, 88 opposed, and 62 voting *placet juxta modum*, which means
approval with some reservations. The minority of two hundred bishops
had been largely won over by the cautious nature of the definition, and
those who were still unwilling to vote in favour found a means of avoiding any vote at all. France threatened war on Prussia, and bishops from
the areas concerned were given permission to return home. There is a
story that some French bishops were in a railway carriage leaving Rome
when one said, 'We have made a great mistake', whereupon his hearer

raised a hand to show that he had already begun reading his prayers and could not speak. If this meant that they had made a mistake by leaving Rome instead of battling to the end, then there is no evidence for it; they might have made a mistake in arranging to change trains in Turin, or the whole story may be false.

On 18 July 1870 the final vote occurred in a thunderstorm, which could be argued to mean divine approval or divine disapproval according to taste. ' "*Placet*" shouted his Eminence or his Grace; and a loud clap of thunder followed in response, and then the lightning darted about the baldechino and every part of the church and the conciliar hall, as if announcing the response.' Finally the results were taken to Pope Pius IX and announced, while 'the entire crowd fell on their knees, and the Pope blessed them in those clear sweet tones distinguishable among a thousand'. Only two bishops had voted against, and they immediately accepted the decree. Those who were absent took longer, but none refused. And the day after the vote, war broke out between France and Prussia and the council was suspended with its major work undone. In August the token garrison of French troops was withdrawn from Rome, and the Italian forces moved in. Pius IX became 'the prisoner of the Vatican', though his imprisonment was more symbolic than real.

It was all high drama, but what it meant was less clear. The Council ended with a lop-sided church; the Pope was declared infallible and everything else was postponed indefinitely. But the infallibility which meant so much to so many was only used once, to declare the doctrine of the Assumption of Mary to heaven, which was hardly a vital question. Infallibility may never be used again. Nobody wants infallibility anymore, with or without *The Times* at breakfast. One historian has said that there is no longer a debate about whether the Pope is infallible, but about whether there is such a thing as infallibility. And the decree that was accepted only says that the Pope, subject to the condition that he speaks as Pope and only on matters about which a Pope should speak, 'is possessed of that infallibility with which the divine Redeemer willed his Church to be endowed in defining doctrine concerning faith and morals', which may mean he is possessed of little or nothing. Again, the four-hour speech by an Austrian prince-bishop on what the definition meant was even more restrictive. General Councils of bishops were to be as free in the future as in the past, infallibility was not personal, infallibility was not to set the Pope apart from the church, Papal infallibility was not absolute, as absolute infallibility only belongs to God, and in some sense infallibility was given to the other apostles together with Peter.

In fact the decree was more limited than the view of infallibility which came to be commonly held. This may suggest that Roman Catholics as a whole wanted a more extreme doctrine of infallibility than the theologians at the Council were willing to give, in which case the Council did not saddle the church with the doctrine, but the church pushed it on the Council. Nonetheless, there were some to whom even limited recognition of infallibility was impossible. In Germany and elsewhere small groups of Roman Catholics joined themselves to the Old Catholics of the Netherlands who had separated from Rome in the seventeenth century over quite a different issue, but their influence was very limited.

So much for Vatican One, which has always had a very bad press and is a useful excuse for everything in Roman Catholicism which someone dislikes. It is only necessary to say that Vatican One was bad and Vatican Two was good and everyone nods in agreement and nobody thinks. The truth is not quite as simple as that.

Vatican Two began much as did Vatican One, but ended very differently. John XXIII was elected Pope in 1958 with the idea that he would not last very long or do very much. He did not last, but he did do. A former papal diplomat, he was not a deep thinker and many of his initiatives were begun without much idea of where they would lead. But he had the right touch. For over a century popes had kept themselves at a distance. They ate alone, and when they walked in their private garden they were not to be disturbed by anything so wordly as a gardener. John XXIII disturbed Vatican conservatives by inviting a few elderly ecclesiastics to share his spaghetti. He detected gardeners hiding behind bushes and told them to carry on as usual. He blessed a passenger helicopter and made the Latinists find translations for such phrases as 'rotor-blade fairings'. He sang the Midnight Mass of Christmas in a prison. He even left Vatican City and travelled around.

He announced Vatican Two early in 1959 and horrified everyone. There would be 2,300 bishops and it would cost a fortune, though at least they would not have to think about kings. Without their bishops, dioceses would fall into disorder. And Vatican One had given the Pope power to do everything anyway, if anything needed doing, which it probably didn't. But those most unhappy were probably the liberals, some not necessarily theologically liberal, but anxious for flexibility in church life, with a new reliance on the unofficial status of conferences of bishops in each country. They feared renewed centralization.

There were four sessions of Vatican Two, each lasting from mid-September until late November, the first being in 1962. The very first day saw bishops rejecting official nominees for commissions to draw up papers for discussion; at Vatican One the packing of commissions with conservatives had been the one major flaw in the freedom of the Council. Discussions on the liturgy soon showed that those who wanted change were more numerous than anyone had supposed, and a North European block emerged as leaders. The old question of scripture and tradition as independent sources of revelation was thoroughly discussed, and two years later the bishops had a document which effectively brought the two sources together and ended some centuries of dispute. On Christian unity the paper for discussion only dealt with Eastern Orthodox churches, and did so in such a patronizing way that the bishops tore it to shreds and sent it back for amendment.

John XXIII died before the second session, which was presided over by Paul VI. The enigmatic personality of Paul VI, and his habit of changing details in decrees worked over by the bishops in open debate, infuriated many. Yet his aim was not so much to block the majority as to win over the conservative minority and thus avoid a schism, and on the whole he succeeded. An enthusiast for reform might not have managed to carry the conservatives as he did. Yet he was not a pope for rotor-blade fairings and in contrast to John XXIII has never been given much credit.

The second session considered a new paper on the church, which was the most significant. Some bishops wanted a new title for the Blessed Virgin Mary, 'mediatrix of all graces'. They knew that back home there was grave disquiet at the bishops having not yet produced a new doctrine, as expected, and indeed having actually argued with each other. This new title would have pleased many, but it was not to be. Eventually they produced a chapter praising the Virgin Mary but adding, 'no creature could ever be counted equal with the incarnate Word and Redeemer'. There would only be one 'Mediator'. This disappointed many devout Catholics, but in the years to come devotion to Mary became more restrained quite apart from the results of the Council. It may have reached its high point because of the need for it in the Middle Ages, when the Catharist heresy denied the true birth and humanity of Christ. It probably became more popular in the wake of those nineteenth-century theological trends which emphasized the birth of Christ, rather than the death and resurrection of Christ. But regardless of the causes, it seemed to have already performed whatever service was required of it.

The major subject of discussion for the decree on the church was collegiality. This was the idea of collective action by bishops, and it was hoped that it would end the isolation of the Pope by placing him amongst a 'college' of bishops raised to his level. It was perhaps a mixed blessing. If it was bad to have a Pope raised up above the rest of the church, it might well be worse to have all the bishops there too. And in some of the arguments for collegiality there was a deliberate attempt to minimize the pastoral functions of the bishop in order to show that if there is such a thing as a bishop then he must have functions, which could only be governing functions. Again, if bishops constituted a college separate from the priests then they must be a different order from priests, and perhaps Vatican Two went too far in this direction. Ultimately the debate over bishops depended on whether they were local or part of a universal college, and this raised another question. Is the church a world-wide body which shows itself locally, or is it a union of many local bodies of worshippers? These two ideas are best kept in tension, but Vatican Two saw them polarized. Initially some would-be reformers preferred the primacy of the local church, as this would allow France or the Netherlands to claim some autonomy in which reforms might be undertaken. But once it became clear that there was an overall majority for reform, there was a move to accept the universal nature of the church, as only thus could the universal college of bishops exercise oversight. Yet it cannot be denied that dangers had to be accepted, and the overall result was one of gain.

The third session in 1964 was the most controversial. The bishops had improved their theological education and were now voting quickly and efficiently. Collegiality was overwhelmingly accepted. But in the 'October Crisis' documents were sent to be reworked by conservatives, leading to a great uproar. In the 'November Crisis' the key sections on collegiality were found to have been given a conservative introduction, presumably by Paul VI, though if this was to win over the diehards it worked. Instead of three hundred in opposition there were only a handful. And when the bishops returned to their dioceses, which appeared to have survived their absence remarkably well, they had accomplished more than in either of the previous sessions.

The fourth session in 1965 tidied up the pieces. Religious liberty was firmly seen to stem from human nature and not from the truth or otherwise of the doctrine held. And at last the Council was over.

Vatican Two may have prepared the church for the coming storm, but it still left many dissatisfied. Collegiality and the principle of some sort of participation at all levels has made only limited headway in the years since 1965. Synods of bishops at Rome have not had much influence.

Ecumenism has been found to be immensely more difficult than it seemed when the non-Catholic observers sat with the bishops at Vatican Two, though it must be admitted that Roman Catholics managed to get into ecumenism just when it was declining anyway. At least there was a new friendliness, though since this was shown both by Catholics and by non-Catholics it cannot have been entirely the work of Vatican Two. And the new Catholic interest in Protestantism stemmed partly from a belief that Protestants were accustomed to secularism and had some sort of resistance to it, of which the secret might be disclosed to Catholics. Meanwhile, the slide in vocations to the priesthood and to orders for both men and women continued. There was radical revision of the whole shape of Roman Catholic worship, but that had not been predicted by Vatican Two, which still expected Latin to be the norm. Yet Vatican Two had laid down principles for reform of worship, and this eased the transition, even if it did not cause it. It is noteworthy that just when the Roman Mass became ancient history, so did the Anglican Book of Common Prayer. The movement for change was greater than either church.

One thing which the Second Vatican Council had left to the Pope was the legitimacy or otherwise of oral contraception. Years went by, and in the developed world millions of Catholic women used the pill, with their spiritual advisers saying that it would probably be authorized in due course. Then in 1968 Pope Paul VI gave his ruling, and it was negative. More seriously, it was based on theological arguments which did not convince. Faced with a furious reaction, Paul VI virtually apologized, saying that he had done his best. Bishops and priests expressed support for the Pope, but after an initial muddle they settled down to reluctant acceptance of the facts. Large parts of the Catholic world ignored the Pope. Large parts of the Catholic clergy ignored the fact that the Catholic laity were ignoring the Pope. Nobody thought of bringing in infallibility, which was far too fragile a thing to be risked in such a dangerous affair as this. And yet there was no formal breach of unity. Outwardly things went on as before.

With the benefit of hindsight, it may be thought fortunate that Paul VI gave his ruling on oral contraception just when he did. It was in the year when institutions and structures were least regarded throughout the whole world. As one result, the papacy was at its least institutional and least structural. As one critic put it, if the Pope shot himself in the foot he did so at a time when he had no foot, and it could not hurt. And yet the papacy outlived the ideologies of the 1960s and did so with its nature to some extent defined by a ruling made in 1968. This could only be accepted if the papacy was seen in the light of 1968. And it may be that in the long run the disastrous ruling of 1968 will have made the papacy less concrete and more ethereal, and thus solved the problems created in the First Vatican Council more successfully than was done by the Second Vatican Council.

17

The Great Decline

Churches in this century have been declining, and they have finally admitted this even if they have not understood it. The result has been a whole string of campaigns to correct whatever has been going wrong. It has usually been assumed that what has gone wrong has been inside the church and so it can be corrected by more faith, more new-fashioned theology, more old-fashioned theology, more good works, or whatever it is that will make the church irresistible to modern people. Behind this thinking is the notion that people outside the church are without free will. They are robots, ready to march into church when somebody presses the right button at mission control. And it is only a matter of finding the right button.

In fact the basic question is whether church growth depends on internal or external factors or, if a combination of the two, which combination of the two. It may be expressed in another way; did Billy Graham make the revival of the 1950s, or did that revival make Billy Graham? The answer to this question will depend on the doctrine of humanity, and variations can be accepted, but most observers agree that external factors matter most. If a population does not want Christianity, there is nothing the church can do about it. On the other hand, if a population does want Christianity, the people will join churches and, if they do not like them, change them from within. This does not mean that churches should be entirely passive. They have a certain leeway within which they can present Christianity to the outside world in an attractive form, and they can usually search for some group in society which does not conform to the general pattern when the general pattern is hostile or indifferent. That this is the case can be argued not just from theology, but from church statistics. In general, when one denomination declines, all decline, and when one denomination grows, all grow. There are differences, but these are mainly the results of differing ways of recording statistics. To those statistics we must now turn.

To begin with Easter communions in the Church of England: these rose in the early years of this century until 1927 when they were 2,390,000. Next year they were 2,339,000 and they continued falling slowly until 1947 when they numbered 1,728,000. Confirmations each year could be expected to peak before Easter communions, and they did reach their peak in 1911, though their steady decline did not begin until 1925. If we look at the Church of Scotland, including the United Free Church which joined to make that body in 1929, we find a peak in 1921 with 1,277,000 on communicants' rolls, which are not quite the same thing as the actual communicants found in Church of England statistics. There is then a steady period, possibly masking a decline in actual communicants, until the late 1940s, when the figures inch up to another and ultimate peak in 1956 with 1,319,500, after which decline is unquestionable. To return to the Church of England, their figures go up in the late 1940s and reach a peak of 2,167,000 in 1956, after which they fall again. And, what is more important, they fall at the same rate as they were falling before the 1950s revival. This seems to be so for all denominations large enough for trends to be measured, and it means that the same decline was going on before, after, and during the revival, though during the revival the decline was obscured by new membership. In other words, a church might lose the three thousand members that it had been losing each year for decades, but if it gained five thousand new members in that year then it was only aware of the two thousand by which it increased overall.

The figures examined so far show that a decline began in the 1920s, though it was temporarily offset by a brief revival in the 1950s, but that decline in actual membership may be only part of a deeper decline beginning much earlier. Some would date it from around 1885, when there were indications that religion began to matter less, and anti-religion began to matter so little that it almost completely died out. If something really basic happened in those years, we might expect it to be seen in London before being seen elsewhere. Large cities provide sufficient anonymity so that people can begin churchgoing or stop churchgoing without arousing the curiosity of neighbours. And surveys, which are admittedly open to question, do indicate that between 1881 and 1901 the population of London rose from 3,816,000 to 4,536,000, while from 1886 to 1901 the churchgoers declined from 1,167,000 to 1,003,000.

But whether decline began in 1885 or in 1921, we still do not know what caused it. There is no national crisis which seems to fit the dates, either economic or political or theological or biblical. However, it does seem that the reasons for people no longer attending church are more likely to have been religious than social or economic, unless we believe that churchgoing is not a religious activity, but is some shadow of economic necessity. Yet even if we hold that the reasons are basically religious, we are not much farther ahead. There is a theory about popular religion. Below the level of 'church religion' there is supposed to be a solid bedrock of 'popular religion', which may be simplified church religion, or perhaps an earlier form of church religion, or perhaps quite different. From time to time the two types of religion drift together, one above the other, and the religion of the people happens to be that of the church, so many people go to church. Then the two religions drift apart, like tectonic plates in geology, and church membership falls. But this theory assumes that people are naturally religious, and some would argue that people are not. If people are not naturally religious then churchgoing is an optional activity and whole populations can go through life without even thinking about ultimate questions. The evidence on this question is mixed, and no answer is final.

If we look at the revival of the 1950s, we may return to the question of whether it was made by Billy Graham or whether it made him. The first point to note is that Billy Graham was not the only notable religious figure of those years. He spoke to Evangelical Protestants, but Norman Vincent Peale spoke to Liberal Protestants, while someone called G. Henry Oxnam was a notable figure somewhere in between, and Fulton J. Sheen was an evangelist for Roman Catholics in America. All flourished for a while, but by the 1960s even Billy Graham was publicly saying that the time for mass evangelism might have passed. And throughout America, where there had been rapid growth in all kinds of church membership, decline struck most denominations in the 1960s, though conservative groups such as Missouri Lutherans, Roman Catholics and Southern Baptists only began their decline in the 1970s. This roughly paralleled the church statistics of Britain and the European Continent, so it is possibly to argue with some degree of confidence that the decline is to be found throughout the Western world, and perhaps even in the Soviet Union. It does not, therefore, come from any particular strategy of any particular church. It is much greater, and we may suppose that its main cause is external to church life.

In the late 1970s there were suggestions that the decline was coming to an end. Some denominations made a slight gain from 1978, some declined more gently than they had done previously, some stayed roughly level. But it seems that the long-term decline was continuing, though it was once more being offset by a temporary revival like that of the 1950s, though a much milder one. Early indications were that the 1980s revival ended in 1983, but even if it did end then, it was still significant. Churches are like camels and capable of going long distances between oases; many churches have kept going for thirty years with the infusions of new members and revived older ones from the 1950s, and the revival of the 1980s may well keep them going until the next oasis, whenever that is reached.

Roman Catholic statistics are kept in such way as to be quite incompatible with those of other churches, but it is generally held that in countries where Roman Catholicism carries a cultural identity it is proof against erosion for longer than are other forms of Christianity. However, when the decline really bites, the effect may be dramatic. English Roman Catholics always assumed that they would go up as Anglicans went down, and the discovery that both were at the same end of the seesaw was something of a shock. Nonetheless, British Roman Catholics have shown themselves very resilient. One type of statistics beloved by Roman Catholics is the number of priests ordained each year, and this can be expressed as a percentage of those lost by death or departure. In 1975 the figure for Great Britain was 73%, which meant they replaced almost three-quarters of the priests they lost. This may seem pretty awful, but Ireland only replaced 45%, West Germany 34%, Italy 50%, Portugal 10%, France 18%, and the Netherlands 7.7%. The only nation to exceed the loss rate was Poland at 175%, but if this suggests that Communist rule is the answer then it is not so. The rate for Hungary was only 32%.

All studies of modern church decline must take into account the revolution of the 1960s. In that decade, and perhaps most noticeably in 1968, and perhaps most violently in May of 1968, the known world underwent a philosophical or cultural shift not unlike that of 1848, but one that soon passed and left little sign of its passing. Some would say that it originated in the philosophy of Wittgenstein and the linguistic analysis school, while others would argue that it was too broad to be the work of any academic. It had something in common with mediaeval nominalism. It held that images are such poor guides to the reality behind the images that they are positively misleading. In one of its wilder American forms it delighted in what it called the 'Death of God'.

This could mean anything or nothing, but usually it meant that the God known to us is just a collection of misleading ideas and now that the old God is dead we can see the real God. In politics it could be argued that all that went on was just a 'spectacle', and if large enough crowds shouted that they did not believe it, then it would go away. Words were suspect. Direct action was to be preferred. And action should be taken without talking about it or, apparently, thinking about it either. Praying without words was suddenly very attractive.

All institutions were regarded as obstacles to knowing God. The church became an obstacle to grace and not a means of grace. God was no longer distant and holy but immediately at hand and familiar. Church buildings which were designed to create a sense of awe were stripped of their furnishings. What was left was something like a badminton court with a table in the middle, preferably slightly out of symmetry, and a congregation dressed more for badminton than for worship. Sometimes formal worship disappeared altogether. A coffee-shop became the mark of a forward-looking church, and then became the forward-looking church. Clergymen denounced their ministry and set off to make pottery in the Arizona Badlands. There was no sense of sin and no sense of duty; impulse was everything. In a lasting change cremation replaced burial; this may or may not have reflected a view that the body was no longer the true image of the person. But if that change lasted, few others did. Suddenly it was all over.

A local newspaper on the fringes of Greenwich Village in New York put it very nicely with the story of an elderly couple. The wife had been shopping and told her husband that on her way back she had dropped into a church. The husband asked what play was being performed. The wife said it didn't seem to be a play; they were holding a service and someone was preaching a sermon. The husband suggested that this might have been a long part in some historical play, but the wife would have none of it. They were having a service. Whereupon the husband remarked on the ways in which the young folk were moving, and on how they as older folk must let them take the lead and go along with novelties such as sermons.

If we wish to chart the progress of thought in these years, one way to do so is by noting the conclusions of biblical scholars. In general, each will be found to be saying what was said in his age by scientists and others. Strauss wrote his *Life of Jesus* in 1835, stressing the use of myth and the way in which the sources were 'embellished by the faith of the church'. This was very much part of the new Romanticism. Ernest

Renan wrote his *Life of Jesus* in 1863 and his Jesus was purely human; this was the age in which humanity was seen at its best. Baur showed that nothing stayed still, and Wellhausen that the Pentateuch came into being through a long process of development and not as a single action. In this century Max Planck showed that we cannot know a clear picture of what is happening, but only glimpses of disconnected instants; Bultmann said that the Gospels were not history but 'reflections of the faith and life of the early church'. It was no accident that the quest for 'the historical Jesus' was abandoned at this time. This was not, as has been suggested, because it was unsuccessful; being unsuccessful has never worried biblical scholars. It was because history no longer mattered. But Bultmann's demythologizing, which began as early as 1941, came to be popular, as it paralleled the philosophy of the 1960s in which everything was myth and the myths had to be cleared away, though Bultmann ultimately believed that you could not communicate without some sort of myth.

In the history of the church the old may suddenly become the new, and the new may suddenly become the old. What seemed to be permanent often fades away, and what seems to have faded is there after all. The church is pushed this way and that by waves and by winds, and yet it never quite goes on the rocks. Henry Scott Holland described it in 1914 when the Bishop of Zanzibar wrote a pamphlet asking where the church stood. Scott Holland said that it did not stand at all, but 'moves and pushes and slides and staggers and falls and gets up again, and stumbles on and presses forward and falls into the right position after all'. That is church history.